50 THINGS TO REALIZE BEFORE IT'S TOO LATE - PART 2

MANOJ CHENTHAMARAKSHAN

Contents

Contents

Contents

Introduction

Hey hey hey! Welcome to the second part of "**50 Things to Realize before it's too late**". After the success of the first book, I received tons of messages asking me to continue the series.

Initially, I thought the title suggested there were only 50 things to realize, but then I realized—hey, there's still so much more I've learned since launching that book! I had jotted down a few ideas in my Apple Notes, and I figured, why not share them in a second edition?

So, here it is—the second part of the book. Keep in mind that I'm not here to teach or take credit for these insights. In most chapters, I share the wisdom of the teachers and sources from whom I've learned.

This book is simply a collection of lessons I've picked up from different books, movies, and the vast expanse of the internet. There's no rigid structure or rules here—just consider this book your honest friend sharing some insights with you.

Have fun reading, and enjoy the journey!

CHAPTER ONE

DON'T TRY TO CHANGE OTHERS

The biggest change from my previous book to this one is that I got married. You know how people say you can't change others, only yourself? It sounds easy, but when you get married, it's a whole different story.

My wife, Sneha, and I were totally different. During our dating phase, we spent about 8 hours together, but after marriage, we were together 24/7. That's when you really get to know someone. I came in with certain expectations, but reality was quite different. There's a saying that the closer you look, the more mistakes you find.

The person you marry, or have already married, is completely different from you. They grew up in a different environment, with different values taught by their parents—things like where to keep clothes, how to eat, when to eat, when to sleep, how to use electricity and water, and so on. On the other hand, you have your own set of patterns. When you both come together to spend the rest of your lives in the same house, problems arise.

It's hard to cope with the change, and then the competition begins over whose way is correct. Coming to an agreement without fighting is tough, but there will be a point of saturation.

It's natural to feel the need to change others. We often think our way is the best way. But here's what I've learned: you can influence others to some extent but not completely. I'm not saying I'm unhappy with my marriage; in fact, I feel lucky to have Sneha with me on this journey. However, there are some differences you cannot avoid.

When I tried to change things in Sneha and didn't see results, I got disappointed. This went on for a year until I reflected on myself. Why was I trying to change her? Why not let her be herself? She will change at her own pace, while I can focus on improving myself.

We often mistakenly believe we can control others. We can influence but never fully control them. Even your children have their own personalities. Even though you raise them in your home, they develop their own likes and dislikes.

The more you try to control others, the more you lose your mental peace and theirs. The only control you have is over yourself.

Didn't you promise yourself you'd follow that diet? Did you?
Didn't you say you'd exercise regularly? Did you?
Didn't you commit to pursuing your passion? Did you?

Let's keep our promises. Following a diet, exercising, or pursuing your passion is entirely under your control. Take charge of your life. The commitment you show might influence your family, but even that's not guaranteed.

Your job isn't to change others but to better yourself. Let them live their lives. You know, you gain maturity and a monk-like mentality not by living in a forest but by living with your family. That's where you practice patience and build a strong mindset 24/7.

This phase of life teaches you valuable lessons and helps you mature. In the end, it's not **"YOU"** vs. **"ME"**; it's what is good for **"US"**.

CHAPTER TWO

WHAT AFTER ACHIEVING?

Both Sneha and I felt a deep sense of contentment after achieving our dreams. So, what now? There was this vast space of nothingness. Not sadness, just nothing.

We had eaten a lot, travelled like crazy, and then what? This emptiness was something I had longed for—the freedom to work not for money but for the joy of working.

Though I still had a few unfulfilled wishes, like buying a Mercedes and building a school, we were content with what we already had. I wish everyone could feel this sense of contentment.

I didn't have a fancy wardrobe or a big shoe collection, but what I had was enough. As I write this book, I feel the same way.

I used to ask my coaching clients, "What will you do after achieving all your dreams? What activities will you pursue after achieving all the material wealth?"

The time came for me to answer, and I had none. I had previously said I would write a lot of books and record videos for YouTube daily. But I didn't do that. Instead, I felt lazy and unmotivated.

I thought that after achieving my basic necessities, I would pursue my passion every day. I imagined writing books, recording videos, reading books, and living a content life. But I didn't do any of those things. I ended up watching random videos on the internet.

That's when I realized that pursuing our passion requires commitment and discipline. We need to take control of our minds. The common misconception is that we don't pursue our passions because we don't have time. Let me tell you, even if you had time, you still wouldn't pursue your passion without discipline.

To start and complete a project, you need discipline. Starting is common, but finishing is rare. To complete the loop, you need more than motivation—you need discipline.

Discipline may sound like a tough word. If you're like me, who studied in a matriculation school, discipline means being quiet, hands behind your back, and walking in a line. But that was nonsense.

Discipline is self-love. Oh, this requires a whole new chapter to discuss. Let's discuss this in the next chapter.

But for now, I need to tell you that it's a lie we tell ourselves that we don't take certain actions because we don't have time. It's wrong. We lack discipline.

So, take control of your mind.

CHAPTER THREE

DISCIPLINE IS SELF LOVE

"I believe self-discipline is the definition of self-love. It's like you say to yourself, 'Hey man, I know you like to eat that pizza, it will feel really good, but you know what? I can't let you eat that, man. I love you so much that I can't let you eat that.' I think the word discipline has gotten a bad name; we often associate it with punishment. I'm not talking about that. Self-love is like, 'Hey look, I know you've got a test on Monday. I know you really want to go out with your friends on Saturday night, but if you fail that test, you won't feel good about yourself.' I love you too much to let you go out tonight. Self-discipline is self-love. If you want to be happy, you have to love yourself."
- Will Smith

As I write this chapter, I'm reflecting on the heavy cheat meal I had at 11 PM last night. I feel horrible this morning. I don't feel good. I could have avoided it, could have said no to my mind, but I failed. I convinced myself with excuses like, *"Hey, it's okay, you're eating after a long time,"* or, *"Hey, you're not sleepy, so let's just eat something to help you sleep."*

Why did I do that? I knew I would regret it. I knew I'd feel terrible this morning because of indigestion. I replaced long-term satisfaction with short-term pleasure.

How can we practice what Will Smith said in our lives? Maybe we can use the same words he used: *"I love you so much that I can't let you do this."* My previous method was strict: *"No, I don't want to do this. I'll regret it. I am disciplined."*

Maybe we don't listen to ourselves because we're too strict. Why not soften it to, *"I love you so much that I can't let you do this"*? This shifts our perception from forcing ourselves to caring about ourselves.

Next day, as I was writing this chapter, I went to a restaurant. I wasn't ready to stuff myself again at night, but my wife was excited about this place in our hometown called **"Annam,"** which serves delicious homemade-style food. I accompanied her but only ate one dish.

I said to myself, *"I love you so much that I can't let you eat more than one dish. It will make you feel bad the next day. So, let's enjoy this one dish and find the best pleasure in it."* My body listened to this affirmation. As soon as I finished that one dish, I felt full. My stomach felt content.

Earlier, I would have eaten two to three dishes at the same restaurant. So, my verdict is that this works.

Say it with love. Say the words like, *"I love you so much*

that...." It creates a shift in our mind.

Why don't you try this?

CHAPTER FOUR

PROOVE THEM WRONG?!

Here are some of the toxic positivity quotes you see on Instagram, TikTok, and Pinterest:

-*"Prove them wrong."*
- *"Hustle."*
- *"Show them how it's done."*
- *"Losers sleep for 8 hours; winners sleep for 2 hours."*

These are examples of modern toxic positivity spreading across the internet. While the drive to prove someone wrong might help you achieve a goal, is it really worth it if it means losing precious days of your life?

Imagine your uncle once told you that you amount to nothing and would never be successful. Hearing this, you felt a mix of sadness and motivation, determined to prove him wrong. So, you started building a business, working tirelessly 16 hours a day. You assembled a team of 100 members, raised capital, and, after 7 years, reached the pinnacle of your business and achieved financial freedom.

You were eager to flaunt your success to your uncle.

However, upon arriving at his house, you discover that he passed away 5 years ago. What now? He isn't alive to see your success. Does this realization make you feel sad, or do you still find joy in your victory?

While I'm glad if you're happy, consider this: was it worth it if it leaves you feeling empty? Perhaps your true dream was to become an independent musician. Had you pursued that path, you might have achieved success within the same 7 years, driven by a passion for music rather than a need to prove yourself. In this case, success would have been about personal fulfilment rather than validation from others.

My point is that you don't need to prove anything to anyone, even your own parents. Everyone has their own journey to follow, and you don't need to justify your path to them. Focus on your own life and let others lead theirs.

In a scene from a Rajinikanth movie, he initially lives a serene life as a milkman. However, his life takes a dramatic turn when a rivalry erupts between him and his friend. From that moment on, he works relentlessly, builds businesses, and competes fiercely to reach the top. His dedication to his career leads him to spend less time with his family. By the end of the film, overwhelmed by business pressures, he parks his car on a mountaintop and stands there, grappling with frustration.

While there, he overhears someone speaking to their cows, saying, *"Come on, let's go home now. Once I tie you in the shed, I can sleep peacefully."* Hearing this, he smiles and realizes that he has been pursuing the wrong path all along. In his quest for vengeance, he has wasted years of his life.

Don't fall into the trap of trying to prove yourself to others. You don't need to fulfill anyone's expectations but your own. Keep asking yourself these questions:

Who am I?
What do I truly enjoy?
What are my strengths?
What fulfills my soul?

CHAPTER FIVE

WHERE ARE YOU RUNNING?

Have you watched the movie **"Forrest Gump"**? In one scene, Tom Hanks's character starts running down the road without any particular reason. He initially plans to run to the end of his street, but when he reaches it, he decides to run to Greenbow County. When he gets there, he thinks, *"Why not run to the state of Alabama?"* He keeps running with no specific end destination in mind.

Meanwhile, the media misinterprets his actions, speculating that he is running for a cause. People ask him if he is running for world peace, women's empowerment, or animals. But he is running for no particular reason, which the media cannot accept.

Months later, people begin to join him. His run continues for three years, and one day, out of nowhere, he suddenly stops and realizes that he needs to stop running. As he turns back, the group of people who have followed him wait, expecting something profound. He simply says, *"I'm pretty tired. I think I'll go home now."*

The crowd is stunned by this response, and someone asks, *"Now what do we do?"*

This scene has always resonated with me. Everyone is on a journey; some know what they want and are moving toward it, while others run because those around them are running. Can you relate to this?

I emphasize self-awareness and self-introspection for this reason. We are often influenced by our surroundings. For example, in an earlier chapter, I mentioned that I had no intention of buying a Harley-Davidson, yet I started working towards it. We are easily swayed by others if we are not self-aware.

Are you running your own race, or are you running someone else's?

Are you aware of where you are headed?

Do you know your **"Why"**?

Just like in the movie scene, we may start running behind someone, believing that they will lead us to enlightenment. While some leaders do help, others are so confused that they cannot guide us truthfully, so they just keep running.

I was deeply moved by this book, **"Siddhartha"** by Hermann Hesse, which tells the story of Siddhartha and his friend Govinda, who embark on a profound journey to discover the truth. For years, Govinda trails closely behind Siddhartha, absorbing his teachings and following his lead.

But then, a pivotal moment arrives: Govinda chooses to part ways and forge his own path. Siddhartha, rather than feeling abandoned, is genuinely delighted. He sees Govinda's decision as a courageous step toward self-discovery, reflecting his own growth and understanding. Siddhartha's joy stems from witnessing his friend's personal journey and independence, embracing the idea that true wisdom often comes from exploring one's unique path. *(This is a portion of the story, not the entire plot.)*

Isn't it mature to be happy that a friend is finding his own way rather than following you? I was moved by this chapter and realized the importance of making one's own decisions and allowing others to do the same.

In the story, Siddhartha does not say, *"No, don't go. You don't know anything; I will guide you."* He does not stop Govinda but encourages him to find his own path.

I have read that even Buddha appreciated people who questioned his teachings. He encouraged individuals not to simply follow his words, but to engage in self-inquiry.

Today, I see so-called gurus claiming, *"My way is the only way."* Some religious groups resist the coexistence of differing beliefs. People who assert that *"My way is the only way"* are often driven by their own ego.

Ultimately, it's about finding your own path and allowing others to choose theirs.

Acceptance.

CHAPTER SIX

EAGLE VIEW

When we're watching a football match, we often feel like experts, more knowledgeable than the coach who has dedicated 20 years to training the players. We shout at the TV, advising players to pass the ball to the left and cursing them if they don't make the move we suggested from 200 miles away.

Most of the time, our advice seems spot on. But how do we become such geniuses, making these decisions while holding a beer in one hand? The answer is simple: we have an eagle view. The 20 high-definition cameras capturing the match from various angles across the stadium give us a comprehensive perspective. The players, on the other hand, have a straight view, focused on the giant, sweaty opponent charging at 35 km per hour. They don't have the same eagle view that we do from our couch.

This vantage point allows us to make smarter decisions. Now, let's apply this concept to our lives. As we navigate our daily routines and face regular challenges, our vision often becomes short-sighted. We focus only on the immediate obstacles in front of us, tackling them one by one. This cycle can continue for years, with us dealing with whatever is right in front of us.

To gain a broader perspective, I practice a technique that involves stepping away from my routine at least twice a month.

I used to do this weekly, and as I write this chapter, I realize I should consider returning to that frequency. My practice involves visiting a coffee shop near my house. In my city, there are four different coffee shops I frequent. I would choose one and spend nearly four hours there, carrying only my iPad and listening to some instrumental music.

During these visits, I sit without distractions and spend time contemplating my thoughts. This quiet, focused time allows me to be honest with myself. It has been one of the most valuable practices in my life. It has helped me make significant decisions, such as starting a company, hiring valuable employees, shutting it down when necessary, writing books, creating videos, and signing deals with partners.

We need this eagle view in our lives. Often, we get carried away with our daily routines and challenges. There has to be a time where you can just lay back and look at your life from an eagle view. If we don't do this, who will do it for us?

I invite you to adopt an eagle view of your life. Take a break from your regular routine. Visit a coffee shop you've never been to before (preferably alone). Commit to staying there for three hours, removing all potential distractions. Reflect on the choices you've made in the past month and how they're helping you move towards your desired destination. Have this alone time to understand how you are playing the game of life.

Here are four questions to help you with this self-reflection:

1. What choices/decisions did I make in the past month?
2. How are they helping my progress?
3. What other decisions can I potentially make in the upcoming month?
4. How would these decisions fast-track my progress?

Spend three hours contemplating these questions. Why so long? Think about how muddy water settles and becomes clear when left undisturbed. Similarly, the more time you spend in this eagle view, the clearer your mind will become.

ARE YOUR DREAMS, REALLY YOURS?

I once had a strong desire to own a Harley Davidson motorcycle. I envisioned it, set it as my wallpaper, and repeated affirmations daily. However, within just five days, my enthusiasm waned. I began to question why my interest faded so quickly. Through self-reflection, I discovered that my desire for the bike was influenced by a close friend who was obsessed with owning one. Spending so much time with him, I had unconsciously adopted his aspirations as my own.

There's nothing wrong with wanting a Harley Davidson, but it wasn't truly my dream. It was a reflection of someone else's desire.

So, are your dreams genuinely your own?

To find out, consider two approaches: self-introspection

and walking the path.

Self-Introspection: This involves sitting alone without distractions and engaging in a deep conversation with yourself. You might use a journal or talk aloud—whatever feels right. This method helps you examine your thoughts and desires more clearly.

Walking the Path: This method requires you to actively pursue your dreams. As you progress, you'll gain insight into whether the dream truly aligns with your interests or if it's something you're merely pursuing due to external influence.

I applied the second method to my bike dream. I began by using a vision board, affirmations, and visualizations. Yet, after just a few days, I felt a disconnect from the whole process.

In our modern age, we're exposed to a multitude of influences—family, friends, relatives, advertisements, mentors, and influencers. Compared to previous generations, the level of influence is magnified. Our grandparents were influenced by a single television channel and a billboard, but today, we face a flood of stimuli from countless sources.

Ultimately, we strive for happiness, not validation. This is an opportunity to reflect on your goals and ask yourself:

1. Why am I doing what I'm doing?
2. Do I really want to pursue this?
3. Is this goal truly mine?

4. How will I feel once I achieve this goal?

These questions are key to self-introspection. They help you understand whether your goals are genuinely yours or if they've been shaped by external pressures. It's crucial to recognize conscious versus unconscious influences. Being consciously influenced means you're aware of the external source of influence, while unconscious influence happens without your awareness.

The essence of pursuing goals should be about personal happiness. Make choices that bring you joy and fulfillment. It's not about proving something to others but about aligning with what truly resonates with you. So, take the time to reflect on your aspirations and ensure they are authentically yours.

CHAPTER EIGHT

GO TO MADURAI

Thyagaraja Kumararaja, a brilliant director, was once asked, *"How does one become a director?"*

Everyone expected a detailed answer from this legend. But he is a legend for a reason. He replied, *"If you want to go to Madurai, you just go to Madurai." (Madurai is a city in South India)*

Did you get it? It may sound normal, but I saw a zen philosophy imbibed in that answer. Let me take you on a journey with this short answer.

What would you do if I told you that if you meet me in Madurai within 24 hours, I would give you 1 million US Dollars? You would do anything to reach the destination, right? You might take a bus, drive a car, find a train, or get a chartered flight. You would do anything possible to meet me because you know the reward is huge, so you would go to any extremes to reach your goal.

Why don't we apply the same philosophy in life? If you want something, you simply have to do it. That is a straightforward answer. How did I become an author? By writing, nothing else. If you want to become a singer, start singing. If you want to become a photographer, click pictures every day.

This journey will take you to places, this action will take you to places that you cannot imagine. My wife once asked me how to get rid of camera shyness. What do you think I answered? I said, *"Open your phone, switch to the camera app, and start speaking."* It was too simple, so she refused. Instead, she started looking at YouTube tutorials on how to get rid of camera shyness. *(You can be a well-known author to the entire world, who has published more than eight books, and been in the coaching industry for 8+ years with tons of accreditations to justify that you are a certified coach, but all these qualifications don't apply at home. Lol)*

The answer is so simple that our complex minds seek a complex answer. I myself got rid of my camera shyness by taking the action of recording and posting my videos online in a series called **"Coffee with Manoj"** *(I speak in my regional language - Tamil).*

It is the ACTION that destroys the fear, not learning about it or researching it. I had this little voice at the back of my head saying, *"You are scared to speak your mind out."* As soon as I recognized this voice in my head, which was my self-doubt, I recorded my voice and posted it on YouTube. A few days later, the same voice said, *"Oh, you are comfortable sharing your voice, but you still have camera fear."* On the same day, I recorded myself with my selfie camera, with no microphone or any lighting equipment, and later posted it on YouTube.

Ever since that event, that fear has never come to me again. I believe in the action. I don't have a million followers, but here I am stating the fact that that's how you get rid of fear—by taking action. If you want to go to Madurai, go to Madurai.

"If you can't fly then run, if you can't run then walk, if you can't walk then crawl, but whatever you do, you have to keep moving forward."
— Martin Luther King Jr.

CHAPTER NINE

LOVE YOUR WORK NOT YOUR ORGANIZATION

I once heard a quote from a former colleague that left me puzzled: "**Love your work, not your organization.**" At the time, I didn't fully grasp its meaning. I believed that loving your organization was the key to pouring your heart and soul into it, which would inevitably lead to growth and success.

It wasn't until I started my own business that I came to understand this concept more deeply. I realized that the greatest obstacle to a company's progress is often its CEO. When you build a company from scratch, it's easy to become emotionally attached to it. This attachment can lead to resistance to change, as I experienced myself. I found myself hesitant to alter our work patterns for fear of failure.

This resistance stems from a place of deep affection. When we love something profoundly, we instinctively want to protect it and keep it safe. It's akin to ships being safest when docked in the harbor—but ships aren't built for harbors. Similarly, an excessive attachment to an organization can stifle its growth.

Instead, the focus should be on loving the work itself. There is a subtle but significant difference between loving your work and loving your organization. When you love your work, you strive to enhance its quality and make continuous improvements. This dedication to the work naturally leads to the growth of the organization.

As Dr. APJ Abdul Kalam wisely said, *"Love your job, but don't love your company, because you may not know when your company stops loving you."*

Here are few points written by Dr. APJ Abdul Kalam

ALWAYS LEAVE OFFICE ON TIME

1. Work is a never-ending process. It can never be completed.

2. Interest of a client is important, so is your family.

3. If you fall in your life, neither your boss nor client will offer you a helping hand; your family and friends will.

4. Life is not only about work, office and client. There is more to life. You need time to socialize, entertain, relax and

exercise. Don't let life be meaningless.

5. **A person who stays late at the office is not a hardworking person. instead he/she is a fool who does not know how to manage work within the stipulated time.** He/She is inefficient and incompetent in his work.

6. You did not study hard and struggle in life to become a machine.

7. If your boss forces you to work late, he/she may be ineffective and have a meaningless life too; so forward this to him/her.

The 5th point struck a chord with me. I used to think that working extra hours was a mark of dedication, but Dr. Kalam's perspective shifted my understanding. Working long hours can often indicate inefficiency rather than commitment. Moreover, I used to justify this by saying I was working hard for my family's future security. However, I realized that my family also needs time and attention in the present, not just promises for the future.

Coming back to the topic, when you detach yourself from the organization and focus on improving the quality of your work, the organization grows naturally. Even if it's your own company, it's important to separate yourself from it occasionally. Step outside the organization and view it as a separate entity. I suggest you read the chapter **"Eagle View"** for more on this perspective.

Sometimes, when it's our own company, we become entangled with emotions. But we must understand that the organization is a separate entity, and we are employees within it. By focusing on delivering high-quality work, everything else will fall into place.

CHAPTER TEN

FOCUS ON WHAT YOU CAN DO

"Don't bark if you can't bite."
— English Proverb

We often lose sight of what is within our control and what is not. Social media has given us a window into events happening across the nation and beyond. We see injustices and foolishness that can be infuriating—like politicians treating people poorly while those same people continue to support them. *(When I say we, I mean myself. It happened with me. I am a sensitive person who gets affected when I witness injustice)*

It can be especially frustrating if you consider yourself an intelligent person; the irrationality can be maddening. But there's a lesson to be learned here: *"Don't bark if you can't bite."* I'm not a politician, and my influence is limited to casting a vote once every five years. Constant anger at these issues is unproductive. It harms my health, affects my family, drains my energy, and wastes time.

I admire activists who fight for change—they're the reason we have clean air and water. As someone who is not an activist or a politician, but still feels frustrated by the state of things and wants to make a difference, I've chosen to become a silent rebel.

Silent Rebel:

A silent rebel is someone who doesn't just criticize or complain about problems but actively works to create change. In my case, I realized that self-awareness is lacking in society, leading to a lack of questioning and understanding. I decided to help people become more self-aware through writing and speaking.

For instance, if you think politicians are failing to deliver on their promises of employment, don't just resent them—create your own organization to hire hundreds of people.

If politicians pledge to reduce plastic usage but fail to act, start a business that develops eco-friendly alternatives.

Or, if you're a movie director, use your platform to raise awareness. If you're a musician, YouTuber, influencer, or architect, contribute through your field. The key is to use your unique skills and position to make a difference.

The idea is to find your role in this vast ecosystem. Just as a jungle thrives on its diversity, ranging from microscopic creatures to towering trees, our world thrives on the diverse contributions of its people. It's the variety of roles and actions that maintains the balance, not trying to fit everyone into one mold.

Focus on what is within your control. Approach it with passion and love. When you read the chapter **"Find your IKIGAI"**, you will get a clear picture about this.

CHAPTER ELEVEN

IMPATIENT FUTURE

Social media platforms have become a double-edged sword in our lives. On one hand, they connect us with friends, family, and information from all over the world. On the other hand, they are engineered to keep us hooked, often at the expense of our mental well-being.

The irony lies in the fact that many influencers who preach about mindfulness and mental health are contributing to this cycle of dependency. They post polished, carefully curated content that promotes tranquility, yet the medium itself fosters impatience and distraction.

Virtual Autism:
The concept of virtual autism is particularly alarming. Unlike traditional autism, which has a variety of causes and manifestations, virtual autism is directly linked to our digital habits. Children, who are the most vulnerable to these influences, are developing cognitive issues due to the excessive use of screens. Their brains are not getting the necessary rest and are constantly overstimulated. This

overstimulation hinders their ability to concentrate, making them restless and impatient.

Think about how we consumed media a few decades ago. We had one television in the house, and it broadcasted a limited number of channels. Families would gather to watch a program together, and there was a sense of shared experience. With the advent of the internet, we gained access to a wealth of information, but it required effort to seek out what we wanted. Now, the situation is completely different. Algorithms predict our interests and feed us a constant stream of content. We have become passive consumers, and our engagement with the digital world is largely unintentional.

This passive consumption has significant implications for our cognitive abilities and social behavior. Short attention spans are becoming the norm, and the ability to engage deeply with any one task is diminishing. The younger generation, in particular, is at risk. They are growing up in an environment where immediate gratification is expected, and the patience required for long-term goals is diminishing.

Can you relate to this impatience within us? The urge to get things fast. I recently saw a person riding a motorcycle while watching Instagram reels at the same time. Even for those few minutes of traveling from the office to home, they wanted to consume random content.

How is listening to audiobooks different from watching reels? I know people who consume audiobooks while driving, and I'm not against it because your attention is focused on one stream of information for a prolonged period. In contrast, when watching reels, we are exposed to new content every 30 to 60 seconds.

This is a serious threat. If this trend continues, I wonder if we will still be able to spend quality time with our loved ones in the future. Will we be able to look into our kids' eyes and be truly present with them? It may sound overdramatic, but just look around you. Visit a mall and observe how people are glued to their phones. You'll understand this when you start to notice the obscure changes happening in our world. It is indeed a threat.

To counteract these trends, we need to take deliberate steps. Limiting screen time and consciously choosing how we engage with digital media is crucial. Simple actions like turning your mobile screen to grayscale can reduce the allure of constant notifications and colorful apps. More importantly, fostering real-world interactions and activities that require sustained attention can help rebuild our focus and patience.

Ultimately, the change starts with us. While we may not be able to control the broader digital landscape, we can control our personal habits and set examples for the next generation. By being mindful of our media consumption and prioritizing real-world connections, we can create a healthier, more attentive future generation.

We cannot tell our kids not to use mobile phones while we carry our own phones everywhere—even into the toilet. **"Monkey see, monkey do."** Let's build the habit of reading books with our kids and spending time in nature. This will encourage them to mimic us and cultivate healthier habits.

CHAPTER TWELVE

RESPECT BUT ALSO DISAGREE

I was listening to my favorite speaker, Suki Sivam, who said, *"The problem with recent times is that people tend to either completely agree with someone or completely disagree with them."* He emphasized that we are not understanding the basic concept that no one is completely perfect. You should be ready to disagree with them and still maintain a good relationship.

Why don't we stand in between? Why don't we say, *"I agree with Person A on these six points but refuse on the other four points?"* We commonly make the mistake of viewing someone as either all good or all bad. This binary thinking is a flawed approach to life. No one is 100% good, nor is anyone 100% evil.

This is a wrong way to approach life. No one can be 100% good nor 100% evil.You may ask, *"Why should I become this person? What is wrong with agreeing with a person 100%?"*

This creates blind loyalty towards someone. When you

approach life from this angle of 100% devotion, you tend not to see the mistakes they make.People who follow politicians have this problem. Just because they like a particular politician, they ignore all the mistakes they make. They even defend them, even after knowing that they are wrong.

Maturity is when you can respect and disagree at the same time.

Let's take an example from everyday life. Imagine you have a friend who is great at giving advice on work projects but often makes mistakes in managing finances. You respect your friend's advice on work projects but disagree with their financial decisions. This does not mean you stop being friends. It simply means you recognize that your friend, like everyone else, has strengths and weaknesses.

This way of thinking helps in building better relationships. It teaches us to see people as they are – a mix of good and bad qualities. It also helps us grow, as we learn to accept and understand different viewpoints.

In the workplace, we encounter colleagues and managers with whom we might not always agree. Some might be excellent leaders but have poor communication skills. By acknowledging their strengths and addressing disagreements respectfully, we foster a more cooperative and productive environment. Blindly agreeing with everything they say would only lead to frustration and missed opportunities for improvement.

In our personal lives, we might have family members or

friends with whom we have fundamental disagreements, whether about politics, lifestyle choices, or values. It's important to remember that disagreement does not equal disrespect. We can appreciate the good in them and still hold our ground on issues where we differ. This balanced approach can lead to healthier, more authentic relationships where both parties feel heard and valued.

I wrote this chapter because of a conversation I had with my uncle, who is an avid supporter of a particular politician with whom I have many disagreements. We used to have regular debates about who is right and who is wrong, which often led to disagreements and even mocking each other. Recently, I tried a different approach. Instead of focusing on how the politician was bad, I first mentioned three good qualities of the politician and then added three points of disagreement.

The energy instantly shifted. My uncle even agreed with some of the points where I disagreed. The tone of our conversation changed, and we had a more productive discussion.

Remember, it is okay to have different opinions. It is okay to respect someone and still disagree with them. This balance is what makes our relationships stronger and our understanding deeper. By learning to respect and disagree, we become more mature and better individuals.

So, next time you find yourself either completely agreeing or disagreeing with someone, take a step back. Think about the points you agree on and the ones you don't. Respect the person for their good qualities and discuss the differences.

This approach will help you build healthier and more meaningful relationships.

CHAPTER THIRTEEN

SPEND TIME WITH YOUR ISSUE

Do you ever feel overwhelmed by your problems and find yourself avoiding them or seeking quick distractions? Instead of running away, it's crucial to spend dedicated time with your issues. This approach not only helps in understanding and resolving them but also leads to better clarity and effective solutions.

Many of us tend to run away from problems, either by trying to fix them hastily or distracting ourselves with short-term pleasures. However, the key to resolving issues lies in spending focused time with them. Research supports this approach, showing that reflection can significantly enhance problem-solving and decision-making.

A notable study by Dr. Kathleen Vohs, Dr. Ronald C. Kessler, and Dr. Jennifer A. Whitson, published in Journal of Experimental Psychology: General (2011), examined the impact of reflection time on problem-solving effectiveness. In this study, 150 undergraduate students were divided into three groups and given a complex problem-solving task.

- Group 1 worked on the problem immediately without any reflection.
- Group 2 had 5 minutes of reflection before starting.
- Group 3 was given 30 minutes of reflection before beginning the task.

The results revealed that participants who spent more time reflecting before addressing the problem achieved the most effective and creative solutions. Those in the extended reflection group demonstrated greater clarity and were better able to solve the problems compared to those who worked on the problem immediately or had only a short reflection period.

This may seem like an obvious thing to do—it's clear that results are better when we sit back, self-reflect, and then take action. But the real question is, do we actually do this all the time? Or do we often jump to conclusions? We're often great at giving advice to others, but when it comes to our own daily routines, do we apply this wisdom in our own lives?

So, how can you apply this in your life? Here's a simple but effective exercise:

1. **Choose Your Issue:** Pick one issue that is currently affecting you. This could be anything from a personal dilemma to a professional challenge.

2. Allocate Time: Set aside 3 hours exclusively for this issue. During this time, avoid distractions—no phones, no social media, no interruptions.

3. Reflect and Write: Sit down with a journal, write the issue in bold letters, and focus on it. Reflect deeply on the problem, exploring its causes, effects, and possible solutions. Write down your thoughts and feelings as they come.

4. Let It Settle: Just as sediment settles at the bottom of a glass of water when left undisturbed, allowing time for your thoughts to settle can bring clarity. Avoid rushing to fix the issue immediately; instead, let the reflection process reveal insights over time.

I personally practice this approach every week. I used to spend at least 3 hours per week at IKEA. I chose IKEA because they offer great food and free Wi-Fi, and it provides a different atmosphere away from my home. Every Friday, I would use this time to self-reflect on my actions, future plans, and lessons learned. This practice of stepping outside of my house helped me view my problems from an Eagle View. I've mentioned this in a previous chapter as well. You can apply a similar method in your life to gain clarity.

Why It Works?

The concept of spending time with your issues aligns with the idea of letting sediment settle. When you give yourself ample time to reflect, you gain better insights and clearer perspectives. This process helps in identifying underlying causes, generating creative solutions, and making informed decisions. Take inspiration from this approach in your daily life.

For instance, if you're facing a challenging decision or dealing with a persistent problem, dedicate a specific period to work through it thoughtfully. You'll find that this method leads to more effective problem-solving and a deeper understanding of the issue at hand. So, the next time you encounter a problem, remember to spend time with it, rather than reacting.

CHAPTER FOURTEEN

I GOT INFLUENCED

Hosting family can be a delightful experience, but it can also reveal surprising things about yourself.

I recently had the opportunity to host my younger cousins, who were encouraged by their parents to spend time with me for guidance on their career choices. I was honored by their trust and felt proud of my role as their mentor. I believed that my advice and guidance would positively shape their future.

The visit started well. I welcomed them, made sure they were comfortable, and decided to show them around the city. Since they were visiting from a village, I thought it would be a great experience for them to explore new places. Everything seemed to be going smoothly until a seemingly minor indulgence—a sugary breakfast—led to an excuse for a heavy lunch. One movie turned into a marathon of an entire series, and a single day of fun stretched into four days of unplanned, lazy activities.

By the end of the fifth day, upon reflection, I realized that instead of being a positive influence on them, they had inadvertently influenced me to become unproductive. While we did manage some productive activities like creating resumes and applying for jobs, this productive phase was brief compared to the time spent being less focused. My regular workout routine and diet were also disrupted.

I learned a crucial lesson from this experience: I cannot blame my cousins for my lack of productivity. It was ultimately my responsibility to manage my choices and stay true to my priorities. The environment and people around us can have a significant impact on our behavior, but we must be aware of our own actions and decisions.

This experience made me realize how easily we can be influenced by our surroundings. Even if you have strong willpower, the environment can sometimes sway you more than you might expect. I personally find that I am significantly influenced by my surroundings. For example, if I don't use work music or keep a weekly planner, I tend to drift away from my goals and tasks.

If you are like me, find yourself easily influenced by your environment, here are some strategies to help you stay on track:

1. Work Music: Listening to music specifically designed to boost productivity can help you maintain focus and motivation. It creates a boundary between your work and leisure time.

2. Weekly Planners: Keeping a visual representation of your plans and goals helps you stay organized and committed. It's a constant reminder of what you need to accomplish. I use a tool called 'Asana', check it out.

3. Hiring a Coach: Having an external accountability partner can provide the structure and motivation needed to stay focused on your objectives. A coach can offer guidance and help you stick to your plans.

While it's important to enjoy time with family and friends, it's equally crucial to remain aware of how these experiences affect our productivity and goals.

So, if you find yourself being influenced by a friend's binge-watching habits or a cousin's love for extended breakfasts, remember this: laughter is the best way to handle it. Just laugh it off and get back on track.

It's important to bounce back quickly. Sometimes, we're too hard on ourselves—we might miss a week of sticking to our diet, and then punish ourselves for an entire year by indulging in junk food, telling ourselves, *"I'm never disciplined."* But that's not the way to go. Forgive yourself quickly and move on.

This concept could easily be its own chapter, but the core message here is to be aware of external influences and to stay on track. Don't let a small slip-up derail your entire journey.

CHAPTER FIFTEEN

BOUNCE BACK

Do you know that sometimes we are so hard on ourselves? You may have broken a promise. You may have done something wrong that you weren't supposed to do. Maybe others have forgiven you, but that's not all. You need to forgive yourself.

If the thought keeps lingering in your mind that you have committed a mistake, it is like a persistent noise in a piece of meditation music. Even though you want to create something new in your life, the background noise continues everywhere. It might affect your performance at work, at home, and even your health.

So, what to do now?

Sit down and repeat the Ho'oponopono Affirmation:

"I am sorry.
Please forgive me.
Thank you.
I love you."

Say these affirmations to yourself. The more times you repeat these statements, the more you clear all the blocks within you. At the beginning, you may not feel like saying these affirmations, but say them anyway.

"Tell a lie loud enough and long enough and people will believe it."
- Adolf Hitler

Our conscious mind may not be aware of the mistakes we committed 15 years ago, but our subconscious holds a record of all the information.

I met a person who went through a breakup 6 years ago. She kept repeating that she had made a mistake in the relationship, which caused the guy to leave her. After 6 years, that guy is married and even has a child, but this girl is still stuck in the moment of guilt.

She approached me for coaching for work. But I identified that it was not work for which she needed coaching; there was an underlying block somewhere in her life. Upon discussing for an hour, she revealed this information. She was not aware of how guilt from 6 years ago was affecting her work.

The moment I asked her to forgive herself, she went into defense mode, rage growing as she stated that she could never be forgiven and had committed the biggest mistake of her life.

It took two more sessions to make her understand how that guilt was affecting her and how she could not live with that guilt for another 50 years. Although she was initially reluctant to practice the Ho'oponopono affirmation, after stating these affirmations five times, tears rolled down her eyes. That's when I realized a block had been cleared that had been stagnant for 6 years.

We all make mistakes, and it's okay. Holding onto guilt and regret only harms us. When you forgive yourself, you let go of the negative energy that holds you back. You give yourself the chance to heal and move forward.

Think about it this way: if a friend came to you feeling guilty about a mistake they made, wouldn't you encourage them to forgive themselves? You deserve the same kindness and understanding. You deserve to be free from the burden of guilt.

So, start today. Practice self-forgiveness. Use the Ho'oponopono Affirmation or find another method that resonates with you. The key is to acknowledge your mistakes, learn from them, and then let them go.

Remember, you are worthy of forgiveness. You are worthy of peace. By forgiving yourself, you open the door to a happier, healthier future. Be gentle with yourself. You deserve it.

We are not perfect. Let's not strive to be perfect; let's just be kinder to ourselves. **Kindness to the world is a noble act, but kindness to oneself is the foundation of all greatness.**

CHAPTER SIXTEEN

UNIVERSE DOESN'T UNDERSTAND JOKE

A friend of mine keeps posting WhatsApp statuses where he makes fun of people who got married. He jokes about how they are suffering and how single people are enjoying life. This went on for years. One day at my gym, I met him.

After a hearty discussion, he started opening up, saying that he is not able to get married. Nothing is working out for him. He was literally sad that he is getting older and has a lot of dreams about getting married and spending time with children.

How contradicting, right? All those WhatsApp statuses were not real. He was simply trying to hide his pain from the world. Did you know that we sometimes use humor to cover up our pain? Well, our subconscious mind, or the universe, doesn't know how to differentiate a joke from an affirmation.

If you want to get married but you constantly complain about the difficulties of marriage and how marriage could ruin your personal space, you will eventually lead to that result. Don't expect a positive life if you are always negative about it. You might think it's fun to make jokes about it, and people might giggle, but remember, you are also listening to yourself.

Life brings more such events that support your statements. You will come across people who are married and living a miserable life. This, in turn, strengthens your belief. This goes on like a loop in your mind. The more you affirm, the more events like this you encounter. The more events you encounter, the stronger your belief gets. The stronger the belief, the more you affirm it to yourself.

I'm not just relating this to marriage. It could be anything. You often see memes like these revolving on the internet:

- *"Waiting for Saturdays like..."*

- *"Other people's lives versus my life"*

- *"Money in my life be like..."*

I get it, it's fun to share these on your status. But your inner self is listening to all of this.

It will be like, *"Hey guys, listen, the boss doesn't like the idea of getting married. He thinks it is horrible and would make him unhappy. Let's work together to bring such events into his life that will prove his point."*

Remember, you are speaking with yourself every day. Make it a healthy conversation. You should read my book **"I am Lucky"**, you will love it.

If you constantly tell yourself negative things, your subconscious mind will start believing them and will work to make them true. Instead, try to focus on positive affirmations. If you want to get married, tell yourself that you are worthy of love and that you will find a partner who complements you. Say things like, *"I am open to love and happiness,"* or *"I am attracting the perfect partner for me."*

By doing this, you shift your mindset. Your subconscious mind will start to believe these positive statements and work towards making them true. You will begin to notice opportunities for love and relationships that you might have missed before. You will attract positive experiences that align with your affirmations.

This applies to all areas of life, not just marriage. Whether it's about your career, health, or personal growth, make sure you are sending the right messages to yourself. If you keep saying you're unlucky or that good things never happen to you, that's what you'll experience. Instead, affirm that you are capable, deserving, and open to all the good things life has to offer.

CHAPTER SEVENTEEN

INSTINCT VS. ANALYSIS

Once, a frog was fascinated by a spider. He watched in awe as the spider moved gracefully on its eight legs. The frog was eager to understand how the spider managed such perfect coordination. He tried to mimic the spider's movements but ended up tripping and tumbling.

Determined to learn, the frog asked the spider, *"How do you move all eight legs so smoothly? I can barely keep my balance on two!"* The spider, flattered by the compliment, replied, *"I've never really thought about it like that. It's just something I do naturally."*

The frog was thrilled. *"You do it without even thinking? That's incredible! Can you teach me how?"*

As the spider tried to explain, it became overly aware of its legs and suddenly started stumbling. The frog was puzzled as he watched the spider struggle. Seeing this, the spider suggested, *"Maybe you should ask the centipede over there. It has a hundred legs; it might have better advice."*

Excited, the frog hopped over to the centipede. *"Master, can you teach me this great skill of yours?"* the frog asked.

The centipede, confused, replied, *"What do you mean?"*

"I find it hard to walk gracefully with my two legs, but you manage to walk magnificently with a hundred legs. How do you do it?" the frog explained.

Flattered by the frog's admiration, the centipede decided to teach the frog. But as soon as the centipede began to consciously think about how it moved all its legs, it started to stumble. No matter how hard it tried to explain, the centipede tripped and fell repeatedly. Frustrated and angry, the centipede snapped, *"I used to walk just fine until you asked me to explain it. Just, get lost. Never come back here ever again."*

What can we learn from this story?

This story illustrates a valuable lesson: we often have innate skills that we perform effortlessly, but once we become conscious of them and try to analyze or teach them, we find it challenging to replicate our natural ease.

As the famous poet Rumi once said, *"Words are like crumbs fallen from a grand feast; they can't fully capture the essence of what happens in our minds."* Similarly, trying to dissect and understand every detail can sometimes complicate things unnecessarily.

In my previous book, I discussed the concept of

unconscious learning, which is about absorbing information naturally without forcing it. When you engage in something with enjoyment, the learning process happens effortlessly. For instance, in activities like dancing or acting, you don't overthink or time every move; instead, you let your instincts guide you.

Sometimes, it's perfectly fine not to fully understand everything. Instead, focus on doing what comes naturally to you. If you're a frog, don't try to be a spider or a centipede. Embrace your own unique traits. By spending time with yourself and understanding your natural abilities, you'll discover what you are truly capable of.

However, let me remind you that learning from others is also crucial for growth. While it's important to follow your instincts, it's equally important to seek out knowledge and wisdom from those who have different experiences and skills.

I know this may seem contradictory to the message in this chapter, but I encourage you to read the chapter **"Expanding Awareness"** to explore the other side of the importance of learning and growing through external influences.

CHAPTER EIGHTEEN

TAKE A DECISION

I want to share a story that happened in my life. It was 2014, and I was staying with my six friends in a cramped flat in Chennai *(one of the hottest places in India)*. Two of my flatmates decided to go back to their hometowns permanently, so we decided to look for a new place to stay.

We eventually found a small room on top of a building, but it had an asbestos sheet as the roof. If you know about asbestos roofing, it's used in small houses, and the toughest part is that it absorbs heat during the summer, making it unbearable to stay in. But since we couldn't find any other house, we thought of settling down with this one.

After giving the advance money for the house, I had second thoughts. I felt I had made a wrong decision. I wanted to tell my flatmates that I wasn't comfortable with the choice we made, but I didn't want to sound like an immature person who was backing out. One day, I thought, if I don't speak up for myself, I will suffer for the next 2-3 years living in that space.

I boldly confronted my flatmates about my dissatisfaction.

They all listened to me, but the eldest one responded saying, *"Ok Manoj, it's your wish. I don't want to stop you. Let's not move to that space."* I was happy with this response, but he added, *"You should get the advance back from the owner."* I replied, *"Why don't we all go to get the advance back?"* He replied, *"It is your decision, right? You are the one who should get it back."*

I was startled. This made me angry and furious. I felt like he was taking revenge on me. I was an introverted person, always in the background, never making a choice. But since this was my decision, I took the bold step of facing the owner and getting back the advance.

I later got the advance money back after convincing the owner. When I returned with the advance money, this person called me and said, *"I know you are furious with me. But I wanted you to be responsible for your decision. You made a choice, and I wanted you to stick with it firmly. That's why I asked you to get the advance back."*

This changed my life. It taught me to be responsible for my actions. I am not sure about other countries, but the majority of parenting styles in India are overprotective. Parents don't want their children to get hurt, so they make decisions on their behalf. Throughout our lives, we never get a chance to make any big decisions.

I am glad that person made me go through this. If not, I wouldn't have quit my job to follow my passion. I wouldn't have married the person I love. I don't know if my roommate knows how big of an impact he had on my life, but this is a lesson I will carry to my deathbed.

Do you take bold decisions? Or do you expect someone else to make decisions for you? It's okay to discuss, but mere discussion often leads to confusion and indecisive behavior.

Don't worry about right or wrong.

There are no right or wrong decisions in life; it's simply a decision. Often, we convince ourselves by overanalyzing to avoid making a wrong decision. Stop the internal chatter of doubt, fix a time to decide, and take that bold step of decision.

Later, take responsibility for your decision. You cannot blame anyone. It is your decision. If there are consequences, deal with them with your chin held high. Be proud that it is your decision. Trust me, this is like building a muscle. The more you do it, the better you get at making decisions.

You don't have to be a leader or a businessman to have this quality. Even if you are an employee, your manager would love to see the boldness you carry to make decisions.

It's not about making the right or wrong decision; it is about making the decision and later making it right.

CHAPTER NINETEEN

GET BORED

When was the last time you felt bored?

Do you realize that we don't experience boredom the way we used to? Back in the day, we could spend hours just staring at a wall for no reason. During my study hours, I would often find myself staring at the wall, my mind running movies as if I was watching a film. I could even sit and watch clouds, trying to find patterns in their shapes.

Even rocks had their own patterns if you looked closely. These were the moments when profound ideas would pop into our minds. Even now, I set aside dedicated time to allow myself to get bored, just to avoid overwhelming my mind with constant information.

I believe we all need to experience boredom. We rarely get bored these days because there's always something grabbing our attention. We have devices that provide us with information 24/7. I remember a time when we used to plan our movie and TV schedules. For example, "Swat Kats" aired at 4:30 PM, and I would rush home from school just to catch that episode.

But now, we can watch anything on the internet at any time. We can pause, resume, or even wait a year to watch it. I think this kind of over-availability has led us to not value things in our lives as much.

Do you think this constant stimulation has caused us to lose appreciation for the simple things, or am I just getting old? (LOL)

Research supports this idea. A study published in the journal Creativity Research Journal titled **"The Influence of Boredom on Creative Problem Solving: A Quantitative Analysis"** by Dr. James Danckert and Dr. John Eastwood provides compelling data on the benefits of boredom.

The study involved participants who were asked to solve creative tasks after experiencing a period of boredom. The results showed that those who had allowed themselves to be bored produced more innovative ideas and unique solutions. Specifically, participants who were bored generated 40% more original ideas than those who were not given time to experience boredom.

This data highlights that boredom can actually enhance our creative abilities. When we give ourselves permission to feel bored, we create a mental space where new ideas can emerge and problems can be solved more creatively.

So, the next time you find yourself feeling bored, don't rush to distract yourself. Embrace it as an opportunity for your mind to wander and generate new ideas. As the research shows, boredom isn't just a void to fill; it's a chance for your creativity to take flight.

I truly believe that we need to experience boredom. So, just a suggestion: get bored. Give it a try and see what happens.

CHAPTER TWENTY

YOUR IDEAS CHOSE YOU

"Ideas of every kind are constantly galloping towards us, constantly passing through us, constantly trying to get our attention. Let them know you're available."
— Elizabeth Gilbert

Your ideas have chosen you. They have chosen you because you are the right person to bring them into reality.

On this planet, there are not just animals, plants, and humans; there are also ideas. These ideas cannot survive on their own—they need humans to bring them into the physical realm.

I've come to understand that an idea will come to you, and if you don't respect it or you ignore it due to negative self-talk or constant complaining, it will find another host willing to bring it to life.

I had a similar experience. I once had an idea to create

YouTube videos based on the movies I watched. I wanted to make a series of videos discussing the lessons I learned from these movies. Even though I was excited about this idea, I didn't take any action. I was intrigued and fascinated by the possibility, but that was all.

Recently, I met a friend after ages. We discussed everything from daily activities to politics, human evolution, cooking, and even dealing with emotions. You know the kind of conversation I'm talking about? Those rare, endless discussions where you can jump from topic to topic without getting bored or tired.

As we chatted for hours, she started sharing some blog ideas she had been working on but hadn't yet published. One of those ideas was about **"Lessons Learned from Movies."** The moment she mentioned it, it felt like a hard slap on my face.

Why? Because that idea had come to me before, but I didn't give it the respect or attention it deserved, so it found another host. Like a madman, I started jokingly pleading with the idea saying, *"No, no, no. Please don't go. I'll respect you this time. I'll write this. Please give me another chance."*

I later explained to my friend this concept of how ideas choose their hosts.

Elizabeth Gilbert suggests that when you treat ideas with respect and bring them into the physical world, your life becomes like a biopic—it grows larger than life and continues to exist even after your departure.

Consider people driven by ideas. They often have no logical reasoning for their actions, and even if they try to articulate their intentions, the true purpose may remain elusive. This is because a supernatural force drives them to take actions greater than themselves. People like Nelson Mandela, Gandhi, and Mother Teresa received ideas and remained true to them.

Rhonda Byrne is another example. She received an idea and treated it with love and care, resulting in the creation of **"The Secret."** Her simple act of taking action has transformed millions of lives.

I wrote a book called **"Times Up"**. Although I had never written a fiction book before, the idea just came to me. I was on a holiday with my family in Dubai. After an exhausting day in the desert, as everyone else was sleeping and the sun was setting over the dunes, I found myself on a seemingly endless highway.

I had my iPad with me, and I simply had a thought. I looked at the sun and said, *"Give me an idea."* It was at that moment that I entered a flow state. I began writing—no, not just scribbling. The story idea came to me, and my hands moved swiftly across the screen.

It's been six years since that experience, but I firmly believe that I wasn't the one writing—my brain was thinking, my hands were writing, and I was merely observing. For two hours, I was completely immersed in this flow.

It's hard to explain what happened but all I could say is that,

I was not writing, but the idea was writing by itself.

However, for five years, the book remained buried in my iPad. I hesitated to bring it to light due to self-doubt: *"You've never written fiction before," "You don't know how to write a story," "Storytelling is a skill you lack and need to learn."*

All these doubts prevented me from expressing the idea that had chosen me. In 2024, I heard Les Brown say, *"If you don't respect your vision, all the ideas, skills, and dreams will come to you on your deathbed, saying, 'We came to you, but you didn't respect us.'"*

This struck a chord with me. I realized that I was holding back the idea due to my self-doubt, trying to present a perfect version of myself. Fortunately, the idea remained with me, not having chosen another host. I found the book in my folders, converted it to a digital format, proofread it, and now it's live on the internet.

The book may not be a massive hit, but it's out there.

I did my duty. Did you?

Are you true to your ideas? Do you respect them? Are you taking massive actions?

(Don't get into the spiral of overthinking, the action will lead you to places, people and events)

"You have a right to perform your prescribed duty, but you are not entitled to the fruits of action. Never consider yourself

to be the cause of the results of your activities, and never be attached to not doing your duty."
— Bhagavad Gita

CHAPTER TWENTY-ONE

RESPECT THE KID IN YOU

(Note to Readers: Before you dive into this chapter, please take a moment to pause. This chapter is designed to be a reflective experience, so I encourage you to read it slowly and deeply. Allow yourself the time to truly engage with each step of the exercise. This is not just a reading task but an emotional journey. So, find a quiet space, settle in, and read each word with intention.)

Imagine, for a moment, a little version of yourself walking towards you. This child is you—innocent, curious, and full of wonder. Picture this little self reaching out and gently tugging at the tip of your shirt, seeking your attention. As you look into the eyes of this younger self, what do you see? What emotions are conveyed through those wide, hopeful eyes?

Take a moment to really connect with this little one. Ask, *"How can I help you?"* Let your inner voice be gentle and kind. *"What do you need me to do?"* Pause and listen carefully.

This child holds within them your deepest, perhaps long-forgotten dreams and desires.

Ask the little kid *"What are your wishes?"* and *"How can I fulfill them?"* Allow the answers to emerge naturally, without rushing.

Now, take a deep breath. Inhale slowly and exhale fully. Give yourself a few minutes to let this child express their feelings.

This is a precious moment, so be patient and present.

Once you have absorbed their words, envision holding this child tenderly in your arms. Picture placing them on a grand throne—a king's chair, symbolizing their importance and value in your life. This is not just any chair; it represents the respect and love you have for this part of yourself. Tell this little one, *"I will take care of you. I will respect your wishes. I will not let my self-doubt hinder our progress."*

Say to them, *"I am sorry. Please forgive me."* Acknowledge the times you might have ignored their needs or dismissed their dreams. Promise that from now on, you will not overlook their desires or let them be overshadowed by self-criticism. Say *"I will respect you and act accordingly henceforth."*

WHY DO WE REPRODUCE?

Have you ever had this thought? Why should we have kids?

What is the reason? Like everyone else, even I wanted kids, but I never knew why. It was simply because I saw a lot of cute baby videos on the internet. But out of nowhere, my wife and I had a conversation, *"Why do we need kids?"*

After spending more time trying to understand the reason, we decided to ask people who already had kids.

I asked this question in my family, and they were surprised. They said, *"That's how it is. What kind of question is this? Everyone has kids, and you too should have them."* After a brief pause, they continued, *"Who will carry your name forward? Who will carry the wealth forward? What happens after you? Whom will you pass down the wealth to?"*

I was startled by this answer. The house I am staying in now was not owned by us 20 years ago. It belonged to someone else before that. Maybe 100 years ago, it was someone else's property. Who owned this piece of property, which I now call home, 200 years ago? Was it a hut? Were parrots living here? Was it covered with a forest?

A basic organism's instinct is to eat and reproduce. They multiply. Nature is designed in such a way that creation happens within creation.

An apple is created with seeds inside it, so it can multiply. Every living being has its own mechanism to create its own species. That's the beautiful mystery of creation. An apple tree cannot question the reason, *"Why should I multiply?"* But as a human, I have been given the choice to question my existence.

My favorite author, Suki Sivam, was having a conversation with his daughter. The daughter was so eager to have a dog. He asked her, *"Do you want the dog to make you feel good or do you want the dog to feel good?"* It was a hard question for the kid to understand, but she was smart enough to know which answer would get her the dog. She responded, *"I want the dog to feel good. I will do everything to make my dog feel good."*

This stuck in my mind when I was contemplating the question, *"Why do we need kids?"* Are we bringing them into this world for our happiness or are we bringing them into this world so that they can be happy?

Most of the answers we got from uncles and aunties who had kids were along the lines of, *"You get bored after 40 years. You won't have a purpose to exist. The kids will bring a purpose and responsibility into your life."*

Isn't that a selfish thought? To bring a life into this world just so we don't get bored? I find it funny how we try to give reasons for our instinctual behavior. It is in our instinct to eat and reproduce, but we try to label it by saying *"boredom, purpose, feel good, responsibility,"* etc.

Know your reasons. Don't bring children into this world to fulfill your dreams. Your dreams are yours to accomplish. Don't impose them on your children. Just because they come through you doesn't mean that you own them. They are born with their own intellect and get to choose how they would like to lead their lives.

Again, I am not against reproducing. I may even have children in the future. All I am saying is to have this self-conversation before you bring a life into this world. Make sure your reasons are genuine and not just based on societal norms or personal boredom.

Understand that raising a child is a huge responsibility. It's not about having someone to carry your name or wealth forward. It's about nurturing a life, guiding them, and helping them become the best version of themselves. They should have the freedom to pursue their own dreams, not be burdened by the unfulfilled dreams of their parents.

So, before you decide to have children, ask yourself, *"Why do I want to become a parent?"* Make sure your answer is rooted in love and a desire to nurture, rather than in selfish reasons. This self-awareness will help you become a better parent, and in turn, raise happier, healthier children.

CHAPTER TWENTY-THREE

CREATOR IS CREATIVITY

"Creativity is God."
— Suki Sivam

The term "God" is one of the most revered and contentious words globally. Some people believe their God is the only true one, while others argue that their God came first or is superior. Sometimes, discussions about God and religion can be as childish as they are serious. Amidst all this noise, I encountered a perspective that struck me deeply: Creativity is God. The idea here is that the creative force within us, which has the power to evolve and grow on its own, is akin to God—not the being itself, but the creative energy within.

Consider a plant: it has an inherent intelligence that allows it to produce new plants. Similarly, all living beings possess the potential to create and reproduce. This energy or intelligence is self-sustaining and exists within us at this very moment. For centuries, religions, philosophers, and spiritual guides have asserted that **"God is within us."** I struggled with this concept until this perspective made sense in a new and profound way.

Why view God as an external entity, residing far away and observing our every action? Imagine a plane about to crash with passengers from different religions—Christians, Hindus, Muslims, Jews. Would gods have a meeting to decide who to save and who not to? Of course not. Similarly, whether someone is Hindu or Muslim, jumping from a 20-story building will result in the same outcome, regardless of their deeds. No divine intervention will save them, only common sense to not jump.

Historically, religion and governments often worked together to maintain social order. They promoted ideas like an all-seeing God to encourage moral behavior and societal stability. While this served a purpose, it also shaped our understanding of divinity in a way that may no longer fit contemporary perspectives. I recommend watching the series **"Hellbound."** Although it's a fictional story, it explores a future where religion takes on new forms and offers profound philosophical insights.

Returning to the idea of **"Creativity is God,"** think of it this way: creativity is what breathes life into us, sustains our bodily functions, and has the power to reproduce itself.

I'm not insisting that this is the ultimate truth, just sharing my perspective. If this resonates with you, explore this idea further. If not, feel free to disregard it and follow what aligns with your own beliefs.

(Just remember to respect others' beliefs in the process.)

CHAPTER TWENTY-FOUR

ANGER HURTS YOU FIRST

Imagine this: if you're holding a hot iron ball, whether you throw it at someone or keep it to yourself, you're the one who will get burned. The person on the receiving end might get hurt or dodge it, but your hand is definitely going to suffer from the heat.

In the same way, holding onto anger or resentment is like gripping that hot iron ball. You might have every reason in the world to be angry, and your justifications might seem valid, but remember, it's you who's burning yourself. By clinging to anger, you're missing out on the present moment. Instead of enjoying time with loved ones or appreciating life, you're letting anger steal these moments from you.

You might not call it anger—you might say you're *"pissed off"* or *"upset."* But regardless of the label, these are negative emotions that block you from fully experiencing and enjoying the present.

Your reasons for anger might be justified. People may have been unfair or treated you poorly. However, maturity and wisdom lie in forgiveness. You don't need to confront the person in person to forgive them. Simply decide to forgive whenever the memory of the hurt arises.

Think of forgiveness as water and anger as that scorching iron ball. Every time you recall the anger, pour some water *(forgiveness)* over it. The process might not immediately cool the ball down, but with persistent effort, the iron ball will eventually turn to ashes. It will no longer be a burning issue but a distant memory.

Forgive for your own peace of mind and for the well-being of future generations.

CHAPTER TWENTY-FIVE

MY WISE TEACHER

I lived in Chennai for about four years. During that time, I was trying to find my passion and thought I was really interested in designing.

One day, I met a teacher. I can't remember his name, but what he taught me stayed with me. His hard disk got corrupted, and he lost all his work. This included 3D models and work he had done over the past ten years. All of it was gone. Despite this, he stood in front of our class, smiling, and continued teaching us the basics of 3D modelling.

I was shocked. I asked him, *"How can you be so calm? Let's try to retrieve the data, send it to a lab, do something."*

He replied, *"My creations are lost, but not me. I'm still here, right? Why are you worried about my work? It's all in my mind. I can create it again if I want."*

Hearing this blew my 23-year-old mind. I couldn't focus

on the lesson he was teaching after that statement because his answer had such a profound impact on me. It changed the way I thought about life. I had always prioritized my creations over myself. But I realized then that getting too attached to the work we produce and worrying about losing it is pointless.

Think of a light bulb. It produces light every day. Wherever the bulb goes, it doesn't lose its ability to create light. It only loses value when it's not used. Similarly, our ideas and creativity don't lose value when something physical is lost. The real power is in our minds, the source of creation.

This teacher taught me that setbacks are temporary. Losing physical work doesn't mean we can't create new and even better things. It's about valuing the process of creating rather than the finished product. This mindset helps us stay strong and keep creating, no matter what happens.

There was a famous cartoonist in Tamil Nadu (I've forgotten his name) who used to draw politically charged cartoons. As the years passed, he had an unexpected stroke on the right side of his body, leaving his dominant hand—his right hand—useless. But he remained positive, even joking that after drawing several **"Strokes"** in his life, God had given him a special stroke *(the medical condition)*.

For a few months, he didn't draw for the publishing firm he worked for. Back in those days, there was no social media to keep track of what was happening in everyone's life. People assumed he would never return and that he had retired. But after a year, his cartoons reappeared in the same magazine. People were shocked, and many thought they were seeing old cartoons. In an exclusive interview, it was revealed that during that year, he had practiced drawing with his left hand—and he succeeded. He quoted that it was his mind that was creative, and his hand was just a tool.

How profound is that?

After reflecting on this, I started to understand the importance of focusing on personal growth and development. Our creations are an extension of ourselves, but they aren't everything we are. By nurturing our abilities and keeping a positive attitude, we can overcome losses and continue to create meaningful work.

This experience taught me not to get too attached to my creations. Instead, I learned to value the creativity and intelligence within me. By doing this, I can face any loss with the confidence that I can always create again, maybe even better than before.

In short, the real value lies in the creator, not the creation. This lesson has shaped how I view life and creativity, reminding me to always focus on the power within myself.

CHAPTER TWENTY-SIX

WHAT IS THE POINT OF ALL THESE?

I've often pondered,

- What comes after achieving our goals?

- What happens next?

- Will I get bored? Aren't we all chasing happiness?

- Shouldn't we just accept things as they are and find true happiness by not setting new expectations or striving for more?

There's a school of thought that suggests everything fades away in the end. But what about those exhilarating moments? What about those awe-inspiring experiences? Have you ever gone on a trek, lasting four or five days, staying in a camp, eating local food, sleeping in a tent with the constant howling of the wind?

I had a similar experience about ten years ago. It was one of my boldest decisions: a solo trip across North India. I still remember lying on a grassy mountaintop, surrounded by millions of stars—it felt like being in a planetarium.

Yes, my life is different now, and I may not see those thousands of stars again, but it was an unforgettable experience.

I think we've taken a pass to visit this planet Earth, much like a ticket to Disneyland. Here on Earth, we have these human bodies through which we experience this 3D realm.

We have the gift of sight, allowing us to see the beauty around us. We have taste buds that let us savor the flavors of food. And we have all our other senses, giving us the full experience of life.

But I think we often get caught up in trying to understand everything and trying to control our lives. The truth is, we can never fully understand or control everything. When we try too hard to do that, we miss the point of life. Life is like dancing—you need to let your body move, feel the music, and just dance. The moment you try to analyze the moves and bring logic into it, you stumble.

I believe life takes us on a journey, and all we need to do is be honest with our instincts. Instead of mimicking others, we should tap into our inner guidance and go with the flow. Deep down, most of us know what our inner voice is telling us to do, but our ego often stops us, leading to self-doubt.

Flow, my friend, just flow. Life will take you on a journey; you just need to do your part.

I once saw an interview with Christopher Nolan where he read a tweet that said, *"My life is like a Christopher Nolan movie; I don't really understand what's going on."* Nolan replied, *"Don't try to understand it, just feel it."*

This, I think, is the essence of life. It's not about understanding everything but about feeling and experiencing it. We're here to live, to feel, and to be present in each moment. So, what's the point of all this? The point is to live fully, embracing every experience as it comes, and to let life unfold as it's meant to.

CHAPTER TWENTY-SEVEN

PEOPLE ARE COMPLICATED

As much as I love people and want to help them, I can't help but feel that they are incredibly complicated. Sometimes, I even get frustrated when interacting with others.

Can you relate to this?

Have you ever found yourself thinking, *"Why are people like this? Why don't they realize they're making a mistake? When will they just act normal?"*

If you look closely, you'll see that every person has some kind of quirk or imperfection within them. Everyone holds onto certain beliefs, habits, or behaviors that may seem irrational or misguided. On the surface, people often present themselves as disciplined and positive, living what appears to be a well-adjusted social life.

But spend enough time with someone, and you'll start to see the mental blocks they carry. You'll realize that everyone has their own set of complications, often hidden beneath the surface.

This is why they say you should never meet your heroes. From a distance, you only see their positives—the admirable traits that make them stand out. But those who are close to them see the flaws, the imperfections that others might miss.

When you shift into the role of an observer, life becomes much more interesting. I'm not suggesting you judge people, but rather that you simply observe them.

And here's the truth: even I am complicated. Deep down, I'm also trying to let go, forgive, and become a better person. When we recognize that everyone, in some way or another, is fighting their own battle, it gives us a chance to be more compassionate.

Not everyone is aware of their own complexities, but we can choose to be mindful of ours and, in turn, show a little more kindness to others.

CHAPTER TWENTY-EIGHT

EXPANDING AWARENESS

Everything changes when you expand your awareness.

In NLP *(Neuro-Linguistic Programming)*, there's a concept that says, *"Your map is not the territory."* This means that what we perceive as reality is only a limited representation of what actually exists. Our minds often preserve this limited perception as the entire truth, which can prevent us from realizing the full range of possibilities.

For example, I once believed that earning $2,000 a month was the ceiling, thinking that making more than that would require immense effort and might not even be possible from India. That was until I attended a class where I met people earning $20,000 per month. Hearing their stories and learning about the possibilities instantly expanded my own perception of what was achievable. I began to apply the strategies and advice they shared, and guess what? It's working.

Similarly, I had a conversation with a school principal from a small, undeveloped town in southern India. Having lived in Bangalore, I had met other school founders and discussed the possibilities for growth, innovation, and revenue in education. But this principal had no idea about these opportunities because of her limited exposure. I introduced her to others in the field and encouraged her to connect with them online. The knowledge she gained was tremendous and transformative.

We often draw mental lines that limit our possibilities based on our experiences and current level of awareness. We think the horizon ends where our knowledge does.

I suggest you connect with people who have reached the pinnacle of your field—you'll be surprised by the insights you gain. Whether you're an architect, an author, or a school principal, engaging with those who are far ahead in your industry can provide knowledge that no college course ever could.

These people speak from a place of expertise, not just general knowledge. This book offers a broad understanding, but if you want to truly expand yourself and reach the top levels in your arena, you need to immerse yourself in the wisdom of those who have already made it. Read their books, listen to their talks, and learn from their experiences.

Go deep and narrow in your focus. Don't just read general self-help books—seek out specialized knowledge in your field. I know that I am speaking against my own books, but it's the truth. While general books hold value, if you want to master a particular expertise, you need to dive deep.

And remember, the internet is your best friend—use it wisely to expand your awareness and unlock new possibilities.

CHAPTER TWENTY-NINE

LEARN TO INVEST

Everyone wants to learn how to make money, but very few people understand how to manage it. The best decision I ever made was learning to invest. Before that, money would come in one way and disappear just as quickly by the end of the month. I used to think that the answer was simply to make more money, believing life was all about living paycheck to paycheck.

Then, in 2021, my wife—who was my girlfriend at the time—introduced me to the world of investing. We saved up some money and made a commitment to invest right after receiving our salaries. Yes, we still spent money on things we enjoyed, but we made sure to prioritize investing before spending.

You might be thinking, *"Oh man, I wish I could do that, but I don't have enough to invest,"* or *"I don't know how to invest; I need to educate myself first,"* or even, *"Investing is too risky; it's safer to keep my money in the bank."*

Wrong, wrong, and wrong. Investing today is easier than ever. Just like buying a movie ticket, you can buy a stock. Technology has made the process incredibly fast and simple. The only thing holding you back is fear. But that fear might just disappear once you take the first step—setting up an account and investing a small amount, like 1,000 rupees or 10 dollars.

Why Should You Invest?
Think about your grandfather. If his parents had saved 1,000 rupees or 10 dollars in a suitcase, and you found it today, it would still be worth the same amount *(maybe a bit more if it's considered an antique)*. But if your grandfather had bought stock or gold with that money, its value today would likely be 10 times higher, if not more.

Money loses value when it just sits in your hands. But when you invest it—in stocks, gold, or real estate—you multiply it.

Make Money Make Money
Right now, you might be trading your time or skill for money. But how long can you keep doing that? If you want to escape the never-ending cycle of living paycheck to paycheck, you need to make your money work for you.

Not time to make money.
Not energy to make money.
Money to make money.

(Note: I'm not talking about trading, which can be risky and often leads to losses without proper knowledge. I'm referring to long-term investing.)

I'm not promoting any app or selling a product here. My goal is simply to help you overcome the fear of investing and encourage you to take action. The sooner you start, the sooner you can begin building a secure financial future. Don't let fear hold you back—jump in and start investing today.

CHAPTER THIRTY

FIND YOUR IKIGAI

Ikigai is a Japanese concept that represents the intersection of what you love, what you are good at, what the world needs, and what you can be paid for. It is often referred to as the reason for being, a purpose that gives life meaning and direction. Originating from the island of Okinawa, where people are known for their longevity and contentment, Ikigai encapsulates a holistic approach to life, blending passion, mission, vocation, and profession.

The concept gained worldwide recognition with the publication of the book IKIGAI: The Japanese Secret to a Long and Happy Life by Héctor García and Francesc Miralles. This book explores the philosophy of Ikigai, combining insights from Japanese culture with research on longevity and happiness, making it a global sensation. The moment I truly grasped the meaning of Ikigai was like an **"aha"** moment—a realization that brought incredible clarity to my purpose. It's not just a simple idea; it's a profound guide to living a life full of meaning and fulfillment.

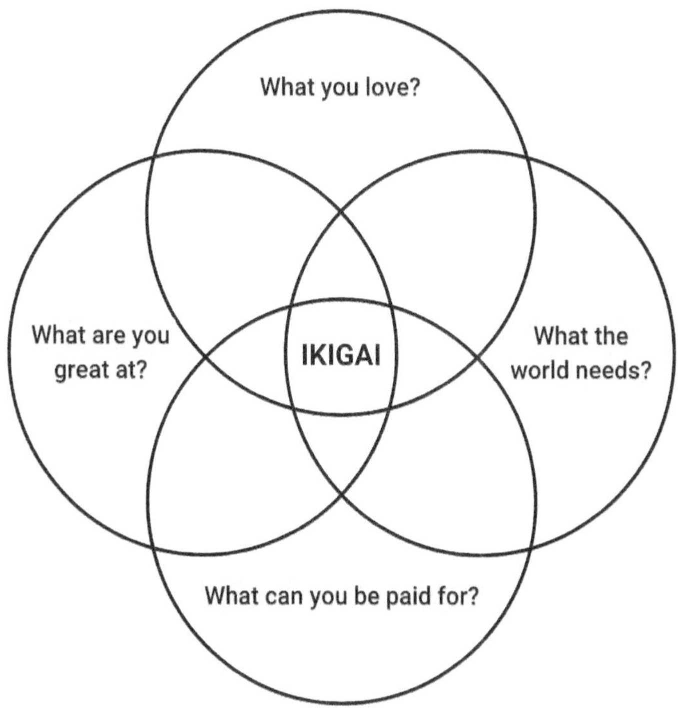

Ikigai is not merely about doing what you love. It's not just about what can make you money, nor is it only about what you're good at. It's also not solely about what the world needs. Rather, Ikigai is the harmonious combination of all these elements. When you align these aspects of your life, you discover a deeper meaning and a powerful sense of purpose.

We've all heard the advice, *"Follow your passion,"* or *"Do what you love,"* but these statements only scratch the surface. In reality, we live in a complex, interconnected world where our gifts and talents are meant to be shared with others. It's not just about *"you"*; it's about finding the intersection where your passion, skills, societal needs, and financial opportunities meet. That's where your Ikigai lies.

What Do You Love?

The first step in discovering your Ikigai is identifying what you love. What activities make you lose track of time? What topics or hobbies ignite your curiosity? Take time to reflect deeply on these questions.

Understanding what you love is the foundation upon which the other elements of Ikigai are built. This is where you dive deep into yourself, peeling back the layers to find your true passions.

What Are You Good At?

Loving something is one thing, but are you good at it? For instance, you may love singing, but is your voice something others would want to hear? This is where you need to honestly assess your strengths and skills.

Ask your peers for feedback, reflect on compliments you've received, and consider the activities where you naturally excel. Knowing what you're good at helps you understand how your passions can translate into tangible skills.

What Does the World Need?

Ikigai is not just about self-satisfaction; it also involves contributing to the greater good. Ask yourself: Does the world need what I love and what I'm good at? How can I use my skills and passions to create value for others?

This step is about finding the intersection between your abilities and the needs of society. It's where your personal fulfillment meets a broader purpose.

What Can You Be Paid For?
Finally, consider how your passions and skills can be monetized. We all need financial stability to enjoy the comforts of life. Ask yourself: Can I be paid for what I love and what I'm good at? How can I turn my talents into a sustainable income?

This step encourages you to think pragmatically about how to make a living from your Ikigai.

The Ikigai Exercise
I strongly urge you to take out a journal and draw four circles, each representing one of these questions: What do you love? What are you good at? What does the world need? What can you be paid for? Leave space in each circle to write your thoughts.

Don't worry about being perfect—just start writing. The more time you spend on this exercise, the more clarity you will gain. Once you've filled in all four circles, take a step back and examine your answers. How do these elements intersect? What could be your Ikigai?

Take Action Now
It's easy to read this chapter and move on to the next, but I urge you not to rush. Completing this book quickly won't earn you a prize, but discovering your Ikigai could change your life. To truly benefit from this concept, you need to do the work. Take the time to complete the Ikigai exercise

before moving forward.

Ikigai is a Journey, Not a Destination
Finding your Ikigai is not the end of the journey—it's just the beginning. I recommend revisiting this concept every year. Your Ikigai isn't a fixed point; it evolves as you grow and change. In the past three years, I've revisited my Ikigai four times. Each time, I've gained more clarity. My Ikigai doesn't drastically change, but it does deepen and evolve, becoming more aligned with my true self.

Remember, Ikigai is a journey of continuous discovery. The more you engage with it, the more fulfilled and purposeful your life will become. So take action, start your Ikigai journey today, and keep refining it as you move forward in life.

CHAPTER THIRTY-ONE

IMPORTANT VS URGENT

I once ran a business where I worked tirelessly every day, handling endless tasks. From meeting with manufacturers and taking photos of products to editing, managing listings, learning new tools, handling office administration, paying bills, and speaking with clients, my days were packed. My wife and I thought we were making progress in the business. We saw some growth, but it wasn't until an experienced business consultant visited our office that I realized something crucial.

After listening to our daily grind, she said, *"CEOs should not be bogged down by daily chores. That's the role of employees. Founders should focus on strategic growth."*

We had mistakenly thought we were dedicating our time to growth-related activities. However, we were actually spending 80% of our time on maintenance work and only 20% on growth activities.

That's when I was introduced to the Eisenhower Matrix.

The Eisenhower Matrix is a time management tool that helps prioritize tasks based on urgency and importance:

	URGENT	NOT URGENT
IMPORTANT	**DO**	**DECIDE**
NOT IMPORTANT	**DELEGATE**	**DELETE**

1. Important and Urgent - Do Now
These tasks are both crucial and time-sensitive. They need to be completed today or this week. They hold high priority and demand immediate action.

2. Important but Not Urgent - Schedule
These tasks are important for long-term goals but are not

immediately pressing. They should be scheduled for a later time to ensure they get the attention they deserve.

3. Not Important but Urgent - Delegate
These tasks are time-sensitive but don't directly contribute to your primary goals. They should be delegated to others to manage.

4. Not Important and Not Urgent - Delete
These activities don't significantly impact your core objectives and are often a waste of time. They should be removed from your to-do list.

However, my perspective on the Eisenhower Matrix has evolved. What truly changed the course of my life was focusing on the *"Important but Not Urgent"* category.

These tasks, while not pressing at the moment, have the potential to significantly impact your life. Writing a book, for example, may not seem urgent, but it is profoundly important. Spending quality time with family might not have an immediate deadline, but its value far exceeds any urgent task.

While the Eisenhower Matrix suggests scheduling these tasks, I have come to prioritize them above all else. By doing so, I ensure that what truly matters gets the attention it deserves. On the other hand, I delegate urgent and important tasks to others to maintain focus on what's most valuable.

Now, I want you to reflect on your own life. Are you merely busy, or are you truly productive? Are you focusing on tasks that are urgent but not necessarily important, or are you dedicating time to what truly matters?

Self-reflect on this topic for sometime.

CHAPTER THIRTY-TWO

FOCUS ON THE ESSENTIALS

One of the best books I've ever read is **Essentialism** by Greg McKeown. This book is so impactful that I recommend it to everyone. The core concept of the book is to focus on what is essential—what is truly important and necessary.

I made a big mistake in my own life by not following this principle. I thought that beautifying my business—having a sleek website, a fancy logo, or a clean-looking business card—would automatically attract more clients. But in reality, what was truly essential for my business at that time was delivering high-quality products.

We often fall into the trap of copying the surface-level aspects of successful companies. We get inspired by their colors, websites, and other aesthetic elements, but we overlook what truly matters—the core product.

Yes, design and presentation do help, but they're not more important than the product itself. I've seen businesses that have been around for years with websites that are far from impressive, but their products and reliability are top-notch. On the other hand, newcomers often try to look good but end up delivering subpar products.

Are you making the same mistake? While customers appreciate a good experience, what they really value is getting what was promised. It's all about setting the right priorities and focusing on what is essential.

So, if you want to refine your approach, I strongly suggest reading **Essentialism** by Greg McKeown. It's a book that can help you prioritize what truly matters and make a real impact in your work and life.

CHAPTER THIRTY-THREE

LEARN OR REPEAT

Do you see a pattern in your life? Patterns often emerge when we face recurring challenges or situations. Maybe you constantly feel like you're out of money, attract the same type of partners in your relationships, or have struggled to lose weight for years. These patterns aren't just coincidences; they are reflections of deeper issues that remain unresolved in our lives.

"Insanity is doing the same thing over and over again and expecting different results."
- Albert Einstein

This quote is a powerful reminder of how true it is that we often agree with this idea in theory but struggle to apply it in practice. The reason for this difficulty lies in our habits, which are deeply ingrained and often resistant to change.

For example, if you find yourself out of money just ten days after your salary is credited, it's not enough to simply wish for more money or blame external factors like society or the government. While these external forces can influence our lives, the key lies in what we have 100% control over—ourselves. We need to take a hard look at our spending habits. If cutting back on spending isn't an option or doesn't appeal to you, then it's time to cultivate new habits that increase your income. Change within ourselves is necessary if we expect to see different outcomes in our lives.

The same applies to other areas of life. If you're attracting similar types of partners who don't contribute positively to your life, it's worth examining the patterns in your choices and behaviors. Are you drawn to a particular type of person because of unresolved issues or unmet needs? Understanding this can help break the cycle and attract healthier, more fulfilling relationships.

The spiritual perspective offers an additional layer of understanding. It suggests that life will continue to present us with the same lessons until we learn what we need to and make the necessary changes. This is why some people find themselves surrounded by negativity or facing the same struggles year after year. They haven't yet moved on from their past mistakes or learned the lessons that life is trying to teach them.

How simple this concept is to read, yet how difficult it is to apply. The challenge lies in the need to change our habits. We may have repeated certain behaviors for years, making them an integral part of our identity. Changing these deeply ingrained habits can feel threatening, and sometimes we resist the change process just to stay comfortable.

As a result, we may resort to buying new shoes, new clothes, or going on vacations, thinking these external changes will fix the problem. Instead of addressing the core issues within ourselves, we try to find solutions in material things. I compare this to cleaning a mirror in the hope that it will wash our face. It's literally impossible.

The process of learning and evolving isn't always easy. It requires introspection, honesty, and a willingness to face uncomfortable truths about ourselves. But it's a necessary journey if we want to break free from the cycles that keep us stuck. Every time we choose to learn from a mistake rather than repeat it, we move closer to the life we desire.

This is why it's so important to pay attention to the patterns in your life. They are the clues that guide you toward the areas where change is needed. By recognizing these patterns and making conscious choices to change, you can alter your course and create a more fulfilling life.

Ultimately, the power to change lies within you. It's not about controlling external circumstances, but about mastering the one thing you do have control over yourself.

You may notice that I repeat the same philosophy throughout the chapters, and sometimes even across my other books. The idea is simple: *"You are the problem, and you are the solution."* Some may find this statement offensive, but let's be honest with ourselves—we can only influence others; we don't have total control over them. So, my conclusion is this: let's take control over what we can.

CHAPTER THIRTY-FOUR

CELEBRITIES DON'T REACT

Have you seen celebrities getting roasted on social media? Even mainstream media used to criticize celebrities, speak ill of them, and create sensational stories. But the mature celebrities don't react to any of this; they simply ignore it.

Behind the scenes, they may want to react, but they stop themselves from doing so. If you've been following the news for a long time, you'll notice that nothing lasts forever, what is a trend today will be forgotten soon.

Recently, a celebrity was accused of being gay, and rumors spread all over the internet. People debated the issue for a few days, and it became a hot topic for a week. During this time, the celebrity, whose name was on everyone's lips, didn't utter a single word.

Guess what happened after a few weeks? A new sensational topic emerged, and the crowd shifted its focus to barking at the government. After a month, the same celebrity appeared in front of the cameras promoting his new movie, and literally no one cared about the previous accusation—it was long forgotten.

What can we learn from this?
Shut up and do your work!

People may speak ill of you, criticize you, or try to provoke you, but all you need to focus on is your work. The general crowd is easily manipulated; they are like short-lived insects that appear during the rainy season. If you become tense due to criticism, you'll struggle to move forward with your goals. It will affect your mental health and deteriorate your long-term vision.

You might become entangled in emotions. Even celebrities are human; they can get agitated and angry. However, they control their emotions, often guided by their PR agencies. They channel their energy into being productive. In our own lives, most of us aren't ridiculed or criticized like celebrities, yet we often run the story in our minds that people are speaking ill of us.

Instead, focus your energy on being productive. For horses, there's a tool called blinkers that keeps them focused. Blinkers are used to prevent horses from getting distracted by their surroundings and to keep their attention on the track ahead. This concept applies to us as well. Don't get distracted by the crowd. Wear your blinkers and march forward.

CHAPTER THIRTY-FIVE

BE KIND WITH YOURSELF

It's true that we often treat ourselves worse than anyone else ever could. We tend to blame others, saying, *"This person or that person made my life this way."* We might think, *"If only my parents had been kinder to me."* Yes, it's true that they could have treated us better—they might have said things like, *"You're not good at this,"* or *"You'll never amount to anything."*

But think about this: even if they said those things for five years or five times, you can do the math. The real issue is that we repeat those phrases to ourselves in much harsher ways every single day. We tell ourselves things like, *"You're stupid," "You're ugly,"* or *"No one wants to be with you."* And guess what? Even if those people aren't saying those things anymore, we carry those negative phrases with us throughout our lives.

What did you tell yourself today? Think about the areas where you want to excel but haven't yet. In those areas, you've probably repeated these negative affirmations.

Why do we do this to ourselves?

We tend to be kinder to others. We wouldn't tell someone to their face that they're stupid, so why do we do it to ourselves? It's likely because of the hurt we've experienced in the past. But how long will you keep using that as an excuse and continue living the same way? At some point, we have to break the pattern, right?

Imagine this: if I came to your house and painted a horrible picture on your wall, what would you do? Would you keep that picture up for the next 10 years? Of course not. You'd remove it, maybe even repaint your entire house. So why don't we do the same with our minds?

Take a moment to jot down the negative self-talk you engage in. You can consider these seven areas of life: health, romance, personal growth, career, friends, family, and finances.

Once you've made your list, write the opposite of these negative affirmations.

For example:
Negative Affirmations:
- I am weak.
- I can't find an honest man.
- My path isn't clear to me.

Positive Affirmations:
- I am fit and healthy.
- There are plenty of honest men around me.

- My path is crystal clear to me.

Write your own affirmations, don't copy it from the internet. You believe what you say to yourself, so make sure you speak kindly to yourself.

"Did you know that the subconscious mind does not know anyone else but you? It has no conception of consciousness other than your own. When we criticize others or find fault, our mind thinks we are speaking about ourselves. That's why it's so important to be aware of the power of our words because often, the words and feelings we direct outwardly can rebound and cause havoc in our own lives. We do these things unconsciously, and most people don't realize that our thoughts and words are influencing and imprinting our own minds."

CHAPTER THIRTY-SIX

IDENTITY OF WORRY

I recently posted a video about forgiveness. In that video, I discussed that the best way to move on in life is to forgive people from your past. I mentioned that if you find yourself unable to move on, the easiest and fastest way is to become the bigger person and forgive them. I received positive responses to this video, but I also got a comment claiming that I am deceiving people.

The comment argued that forgiving people is not easy, that we should not forgive those who have wronged us, and that I am spreading false messages. I don't usually reply to comments, but this one prompted me to respond.

Through a few back-and-forth exchanges, I learned that this person had experienced betrayal by a partner. He was hurt and resisted forgiving this person. I tried to explain the importance of moving forward and having faith in the future. However, he was adamant that it is impossible for anyone to move on. I gave examples of people who overcame years of physical abuse and trauma, but he dismissed these as mere stories and not real. Eventually, I stopped replying because he was too attached to his current identity of pain.

I realized that this person is in a state of denial. Even if he needs help at the moment, he would reject anything that comes his way. We all go through phases of denial when we are deeply hurt.

I'm not saying that it is easy to go through what he has experienced. Of course, it is tough and creates trauma. People might stop trusting anyone and build walls to block others from entering their trust zone.

These individuals are hooked to the identity of worry. What do I mean by that? By staying in the worry zone for a long time, they become attached to that identity. If you try to remove it, they may get offended. It's as if the pain provides a sense of comfort, making them resist change. This is a dangerous zone where a person knows they are in pain but refuses to come out of it.

I met someone with a similar experience. He went through a breakup with a girl he was deeply emotionally attached to. Six years after the breakup, where they are no longer in contact, he still believes that all girls are the same and that they are untrustworthy. He hasn't forgiven himself or her.

That girl has married and moved on with her life, but he is still stuck in the past and unable to trust anyone.

People often get offended when this topic is discussed. They say things like, *"You don't know the pain,"* *"You didn't go through it,"* or *"My pain is different from yours."* Often, they cling to their pain as if their identity is attached to it.

Compare this with your own life. If you have read these chapters, you understand the importance of forgiveness. Forgiving is a way to cut ties with the past. It may be hard, but once you do it, life will never be the same. Take your time to heal, but when you have dealt with the emotion,

forgive them. Forgive them because you deserve a beautiful life.

CHAPTER THIRTY-SEVEN

DO YOU REALLY WANT TO RETIRE?

Do you want to retire, or do you want more time to do what you enjoy?

Because retirement can be haunting, and early retirement can be even more so. One of my friends *(he asked me not to mention his name)*, after making millions of dollars, acquiring a luxurious car, and owning a property on a hilltop, went through a dark phase.

He didn't know what to do with his life. He thought that acquiring all these material possessions would fulfill his desires, but it didn't last even for a few days, he said. There was no reason to wake up; he used to lie in bed until 10 a.m. He started gaining weight, feeling miserable, and began to believe he didn't amount to anything.

During this phase, we had deep conversations about finding

purpose and similar topics. At that time, I was very focused on the idea of retiring early and making big money. When he shared his experience, it shattered my belief. He said that retirement may suit certain individuals but not everyone. People who have been in constant progress for 10 to 15 years cannot easily handle the sudden halt.

Don't worry; it only took him two months to bounce back and start a new company. He has since built a strong team and is moving to the USA permanently.

I'm not saying this to scare you but to encourage you to experience the outcome before wishing for it. Close your eyes and imagine your life after retirement. What would you do?

You might say you want to do this or that, travel here, buy that, and so on. But I would ask you, what after that? You might reply that you'll buy something for others or do things for others. Again, I would ask, what after that?

Repeat this question seven times: *"What after that?"* What would your answer be?

What would your routine be? What would you do on a daily basis?

Take a few minutes to think about this question now.

With the answer you've derived, could you start doing that today?

Ask yourself: *"How can I incorporate this into my daily life starting from today?"*

Trust me, I know people who do this, and the success and happiness they achieve in their lives are immeasurable. Life is too short to wait for retirement. Start doing what you want to do, from today.

CHAPTER THIRTY-EIGHT

RAISING STANDARDS

"If you want to change your life, raise your standards."
- Tony Robbins

This statement lingered in my mind for a long time, prompting me to reflect deeply on its meaning. When I started applying this principle to my life, I realized that I had been unconsciously settling for less than what I truly desired. I had set a limit on what I thought I could achieve, based on a subconscious belief about what I deserved or was meant to have.

In the past, whenever I set goals or planned for the future, there was a part of me that thought, *"That's not me. That's the disciplined Manoj—the one who invests before spending, follows a strict routine, and tackles challenges head-on."* There was a clear distinction between the person I aspired to be and the person I currently was.

For real change to occur, it's crucial that I raise my standards. I cannot expect to see transformation in my external circumstances if I don't first make changes internally. Tony Robbins outlines four levels of standards in one of his videos titled **"Raise Your Standards"**.

Most of us reading this book might fall into the **"Good"** category. We do a good job, maintain good relationships, and perform well socially. But as Robbins explains, when you are merely good at something, you may expect good results, yet often you get poor results. This is because the world doesn't operate on mediocrity; it demands excellence.

To achieve truly good results, you need to stretch yourself and go beyond what is comfortable. To achieve good results, Robbins explains, you need to do **"Extraordinary work"**. Imagine being extraordinary at the gym—consistent, pushing yourself, following a healthy diet. It's obvious that this kind of commitment will yield good results. But if you want extraordinary results, Robbins argues, you must start doing **"Outstanding work"**.

Reflect on this: Are you doing a good job, an extraordinary job, or an outstanding job? How can you elevate your efforts to the extraordinary level?

What does extraordinary work mean to you? The core idea here is to raise your standards.

Joe Dispenza puts this idea in simple terms: *"Your personality creates your personal reality."* It's a straightforward yet profound statement. Take a moment to reflect on it again.

What is your personality? What do you value most? If someone else were to describe you, how would they portray you?

Both Robbins' and Dispenza's quotes highlight the importance of our self-perception. In a previous chapter, I referenced Roxie's insight: *"You attract what you think your self-worth is."*

Consider this: What do you believe about your self-worth? Do you feel you deserve the success, wealth, or happiness you desire? If you want to be healthy, do you believe you deserve a healthy body? If you seek a fulfilling relationship, do you feel worthy of a loving partnership?

How you view yourself is crucial. Your internal beliefs and self-worth significantly impact your external reality.

The Law of Attraction supports this notion by stating that when you elevate your energy, you attract experiences that resonate with that elevated state. When you raise your standards, you align your energy with higher possibilities and attract opportunities that match this new frequency.

In practice, raising your standards means setting higher expectations for yourself and your life. It involves not just wishing for change but actively pursuing it by holding yourself accountable to these elevated standards. If you want to see different results, you must first become a different person. This shift starts from within, with a transformation in how you see yourself and what you believe you deserve.

By continually challenging yourself to meet higher standards, you push beyond your comfort zone and open yourself to greater possibilities.

I once had a friend who found a new partner every six months. She would date for a while and then completely ignore him. As we discussed this pattern, I came to understand that when she became emotionally attached to someone and realized he was genuinely good-hearted, she would avoid him completely.

Deep down, she believed she wasn't worthy of such a good guy. Although she longed for a good partner, she unconsciously rejected him because of her internal conflict. I suggested she meet a coach to work through this issue, as she might otherwise reject her ideal partner due to her unresolved beliefs.

So, ask yourself today: What standards are you setting for yourself? Are they aligned with your true potential? Raise your standards, and watch how your life begins to change in extraordinary ways.

CHAPTER THIRTY-NINE

OBSERVING THOUGHTS LIKE PASSING CARS

Imagine this: Every day, we receive a stream of thoughts. Some of these thoughts are positive, motivating us to take action and lift our spirits. Others are negative, pulling us into a downward spiral and making us feel low.

What often happens is that we start riding along with these thoughts, losing sight of the fact that they are merely thoughts. To illustrate this, think of your thoughts as vehicles on a road. There are SUVs, mini cars, motorcycles, each representing different kinds of thoughts. You are sitting at the side of the road, watching these vehicles pass by.

Instead of simply observing, we often hop into a vehicle, traveling far with it, only to realize later that we've gone on a detour. Alternatively, we might try to stop all the vehicles, directing traffic and trying to control which thoughts should come and go. This can be incredibly draining, as there are thousands of vehicles lined up, and you can't possibly manage them all.

So, what can you do?
Sit at the side of the road and just observe the vehicles. Don't get into any of them; just watch them pass by. When you do this, you separate yourself from the thoughts, becoming the awareness that witnesses them.

A common mistake is to hop into a vehicle and then define our entire lives by the journey. Have you noticed people who say, *"I am always angry, I am an angry person"*?

If you ask them, *"Are you always angry?"*

They might reply, *"Yes, I am always angry"*

"Were you angry when you brushed your teeth?"

The response might be, *"No."*

"Were you angry while making coffee?"

The response might be, *"Not really."*

"Were you angry while sleeping?"

The answer would likely be, *"No, I was just sleeping."*

So, they're not always angry but only during certain times. What is that duration?

The person might think and say, *"I'm angry when I'm around people, but not all the time."*

"Were you angry with your child today?"

They might respond, *"Not really. I was kind to her. I'm mostly angry with my wife and some colleagues."*

What can we learn from this? We often define our lives by saying, *"I am always like this"* or *"I am always like that."* But in reality, we can never be angry, sad, or frustrated all the time. Emotions come and go like passing cars. When you choose not to hop on any of them, they will stay for a while and then leave. Reflect on which **"Car"** you were riding yesterday.

This awareness will set you free. The concept of I am not my thoughts, might be challenging to grasp, but visualizing them as moving cars and seeing yourself as the person on the side of the road can make it easier to understand. Headspace has a video on youtube on, check it out.

Title - Quick Meditation: Changing Perspective

CHAPTER FORTY

ELDERS ARE NOT ALWAYS RIGHT

This chapter might resonate more deeply with those from Indian backgrounds, but the essence of the message is universal. It's a challenging topic to address, but it's one that needs to be spoken about: No, elders are not always right. In many cultures, including Indian, there's a long-standing belief that elders should be respected and their words accepted as truth. While respect is important, it doesn't mean that elders are infallible.

Take parents, for instance. Many people are unaware that parents often unintentionally transfer their insecurities, fears, and anxieties to their children. This concept is supported by the Adverse Childhood Experiences (ACEs) study, a landmark research project that has shown how the experiences we have in childhood—often shaped by our parents—can have profound effects on our mental and emotional health in adulthood. The ACEs study highlights various forms of childhood trauma, such as emotional, physical, and sexual abuse, as well as neglect, which often stem from parental behavior.

This is not to suggest that parents deliberately inflict harm. Most parents do their best with the tools and understanding they have. However, they may carry unresolved traumas and emotional wounds from their own lives, which they unconsciously pass on to their children. These traumas can manifest in various ways, from harsh disciplinary practices to unrealistic expectations or emotional neglect. It's essential to acknowledge that while we should respect our parents, we must also recognize that they, too, can make mistakes.

So, what should we do about this? The first step is to address and heal our own traumas. It's unlikely that we can change our parents or other elders, especially if they are set in their ways. However, we have complete control over our own healing. By understanding the impact of our childhood experiences and actively working to resolve any lingering issues, we can break the cycle of trauma.

In Indian religious texts, particularly those from South India, there's a powerful example of this concept in the story of Lord Murugan, the god who opposed his own father, Lord Shiva, when he believed his father was wrong. In a competition between Lord Murugan and his brother, Lord Ganesha, it was decided that whoever circled the world first would be awarded a fruit. Murugan, with his peacock, embarked on a journey around the world.

Meanwhile, Ganesha simply circled their parents, symbolically representing the world, and was given the fruit. Upon his return, Murugan was outraged by what he perceived as an unfair act and condemned his father. This story teaches that even the highest authority, even a god, can be wrong, and it's okay to question and disagree when something doesn't feel right.

Such mature ideologies were once integral to Hinduism but seem to have been forgotten over time. It's time to revive these teachings and bring them back to the forefront.

As you reflect on these ideas, consider your own children or the future generations yet to be born. To ensure that we don't pass down our unresolved traumas to them, we must first clear them from our own minds. Respect your elders, but also know when to respectfully disagree. In doing so, you contribute to a healthier, more balanced legacy for the generations that follow.

CHAPTER FORTY-ONE

THE POWER OF SHOWING UP

It's been months since I began writing this book. I knew that dedicating just 2 hours per day would help me publish it within 30 days. Yet, I kept telling myself, *"I'll write when I get an idea."*

This mindset led to delays. However, I once heard a famous writer say, *"Just show up, and the idea will come."*

I experienced this first hand recently. The three chapters above were written in a single sitting, taking just 18 minutes to draft. That's all it took to get the rough draft down.

Before those 18 minutes, I spent time staring at the blank Word document. The first two minutes were silent, with no useful thoughts. But by the third minute, a small idea began to form. As I started to write, the chapters flowed effortlessly. This phenomenon is known as the *"flow state."*

As an author, my task is simple: sit at my desk and stare at the blinking cursor in Google Docs for 2 to 5 minutes, and then the ideas start to flow.

Yet, we often find ourselves saying things like, *"Oh, not now," "Maybe I'll look up the internet for some inspiration," "Maybe Instagram has some ideas," "Maybe YouTube will spark something," or "Maybe this isn't the right time; I'll do it this evening."*

"BULLSH*T"

This is where the importance of discipline comes into play. Discipline means doing things even when we don't feel like it.

You might get a brilliant idea, but it can quickly fade away over a few days. Motivation is fleeting, but discipline is consistent.

So, my advice is simple: just show up.

- Even if you don't want to go jogging, just put on your shoes and stand outside the house.

- Even if you don't feel like working, just sit at your desk and stare at your work.

- Even if you don't feel motivated, just show up.

Something magical happens when you show up.

Try this in your life!

CHAPTER FORTY-TWO

LET SMALL BOMBS BURST

Ever since marriage, life has been full of lessons. As I've mentioned before, living with a completely new person brings its own set of challenges. Managing our own emotions is hard enough, but now we also have to navigate another person's feelings. I deeply admire people who have kids—I can only imagine the rollercoaster ride they're on! Jokes aside, something profound happened in our life that taught us an important lesson.

We found ourselves fighting over the silliest things—so trivial that we couldn't even explain them to others. After a few hours, we'd look back and wonder why we were even fighting in the first place. Upon deeper introspection, we realized that these fights weren't really about those silly issues. Instead, they were the result of an accumulation of many small, unresolved matters.

This is why addressing problems as they arise is such a good strategy. It's like dealing with a slow-ticking bomb—the more unresolved issues you store away, the greater the chance that everything will explode at once. All it takes is a little spark to set it off.

Do the Ritual

I've mentioned this ritual in my other book, **"Happy Couple."** It's a simple practice that, when done with your partner, yields profound results.

Set aside an hour of uninterrupted time and space for both of you to do this ritual. One person will go first and ask these three questions:

1. What went well in our relationship last month?
2. What didn't go well in our relationship last month?
3. How can we improve our relationship?

The other person listens in complete silence, without interrupting. Once the first person finishes, it's the other person's turn to ask the same three questions.

What Happens When You Do This?

Slow Bursts:

All the small problems that occurred during the month are addressed right away. By resolving them early, you prevent them from building up and leading to a major outburst later on.

Express:

This ritual creates a safe space for communication. Your partner might be someone who finds it difficult to express their feelings. This ritual gives them the opportunity to speak out in a calm and supportive environment.

Listening Skills:
We often jump to conclusions before fully understanding the issue. This ritual encourages us to stay calm and truly listen. It not only allows the person speaking to express themselves, but also teaches the listener patience and attentiveness.

Understanding Their Needs:
What is important to one person might not hold the same value for the other. This ritual gives each person a chance to communicate their values and priorities. For example, you might prioritize cleanliness in the house, while your partner might not see it as a top concern. Discussing this calmly helps both of you understand each other better.

End of Assumption:
This might be the most important benefit of the ritual. In relationships, we often expect the other person to read our minds and behave in a certain way without us having to say anything. But the other person may have no idea they're doing something wrong. This ritual puts an end to the assumption game by encouraging open and honest communication.

By letting "**small bombs**" burst through regular, honest conversations, you can prevent bigger explosions down the line. It's all about addressing issues while they're still manageable and building a stronger, more understanding relationship in the process.

CHAPTER FORTY-THREE

NO ONE REALLY KNOWS

We often believe that we must have everything figured out before we can start—whether it's a project, a business, or any significant life decision. We think we need full clarity and a detailed plan to ensure success. However, when I had the opportunity to meet with CEOs and founders of various organizations, I came to a profound realization: they are just like everyone else. These leaders, who seem to have it all together, are often filled with doubts, uncertainties, and questions. They, too, struggle with unclear paths and have had to change their strategies numerous times.

From the outside, it's easy to perceive them as perfect—individuals who know exactly what steps to take over the next five years. We imagine that they possess some secret formula for success, a clear roadmap that guarantees their progress. But the truth is, even the most successful leaders are uncertain. They don't have all the answers, and they don't always know how things will turn out. What sets them apart, however, is their willingness to take risks and move forward despite the unknowns. They're not paralyzed by fear; instead, they embrace it. They may not have a foolproof plan, but they are deeply aware of their purpose—their "**Why.**"

This concept is beautifully articulated by Simon Sinek in his book "**Start with Why**". Sinek explains that true leaders focus on their "**Why,**" the core reason behind their actions. In contrast, amateurs often fixate on the "**What**"—the specific tasks or objectives at hand. When your "**Why**" is clear and strong, it becomes a guiding force, helping you navigate through uncertainty and discover countless ways to reach your destination.

The insight here is powerful: you don't need to have every detail figured out before you begin. The belief that you must wait for complete clarity is a myth that holds many people back. The reality is, clarity often comes through action. By starting with what you have and where you are, you create momentum. Each step forward brings new insights, and with those insights, your path becomes clearer.

Think about the entrepreneurs, innovators, and leaders you admire. They didn't wait until they had a perfect plan; they started with a vision, a passion, or an idea. They learned, adapted, and improved as they went along. The journey itself is a teacher, offering lessons that you can't gain from simply planning and theorizing.

So, don't stop yourself from moving forward just because you don't have all the answers. Begin with what you know, even if it's just a small part of the bigger picture. Take action, even if it's a little uncertain.

Remember, no one really knows everything before they start. The people who succeed are the ones who are willing to take the first step, even when the destination isn't fully visible. They trust that as long as they keep moving, the way forward will eventually reveal itself. So take that first step. You will learn, grow, and get better as you journey forward. And in the end, you'll realize that the clarity you were seeking was something you had to create, not something you had to wait for.

"You can't connect the dots looking forward; you can only connect them looking backwards. So you have to trust that the dots will somehow connect in your future."
\- Steve Jobs

CHAPTER FORTY-FOUR

WHATEVER WORKS FOR YOU

Some people are really tough to argue with. They always seem to have a counterpoint ready, no matter what you say. You might want to help them, but they've built such strong walls around their beliefs that it's hard to break through. For these situations, the best response might be: **"Whatever works for you."**

I had a friend who was trying hard to break into the film industry. He faced countless obstacles and struggles, and over time, he started to build a wall around himself. He began to believe that life was tough, people couldn't be trusted, and true love didn't exist. His experiences made him see the world through a negative lens.

He began to criticize everything around him. Every movie he watched was dissected for flaws, and he pointed out mistakes instead of appreciating the artistry. He wasn't always like this—he used to be enthusiastic about films and admired directors and actors. But as his struggles grew, so did his bitterness.

One day, during a conversation, he started complaining about directors. I noticed his negativity and pointed it out. I told him that his new habit of finding faults was damaging and unhealthy. I tried to explain how constant negativity could harm his well-being and future. But he was set in his ways, justifying his critical attitude as necessary for survival in the film industry.

After a while, I decided to say, *"Whatever works for you. If you think this attitude makes you happy, continue with it."* He responded by saying that he wasn't happy being this way but felt it was the only way. I didn't push further, I just said *"Whatever works for you"*. This made him think if he is having a healthy conversation with himself or not. I suggested him to read the book **"The Power of Your Subconscious Mind"**.

A week later, he was excited about the book and couldn't stop talking about the ideas he was learning. He began to see things differently and even started sharing his new insights with me. So, what caused this shift?

The phrase *"Whatever works for you"* allowed him to step back from his rigid beliefs. Sometimes, when people are stuck in their ways, no amount of argument or advice will change their minds. By acknowledging their viewpoint and letting them know it's okay to have their own approach, you give them the space to reconsider their choices on their own terms.

I also tried this approach with a comment on one of my YouTube videos. Someone was arguing against the idea of forgiveness, saying it was impossible to forgive certain wrongs. I responded with, *"Whatever works for you. If you believe holding onto anger is what's best for you, that's your choice."* This response allowed the person to reflect on their stance without feeling attacked.

People often cling to their pain or negative beliefs because they feel comfortable with them, even if they're harmful. My friend's negativity had become so ingrained that he resisted any suggestion to change, even if it meant staying unhappy. This kind of attachment to negative beliefs is common; it feels familiar and safe, even if it's painful.

Think about your own experiences. When you encounter someone who's set in their beliefs, instead of arguing, try saying, *"Whatever works for you."* This approach shows respect for their perspective while giving them a chance to think about whether their current approach is really benefiting them.

Using this phrase can help avoid pointless arguments and preserve your energy. It encourages people to reflect on their choices and whether those choices are truly making them happy.

"Whatever works for you" isn't just a polite way to end a conversation; it's a way to gently prompt someone to consider their own happiness and choices. It respects their right to their views while encouraging them to think about whether those views are truly serving their well-being.

So, next time you find yourself debating with someone who is set in their ways, use this phrase. It might not change their mind right away, but it could help them start to reflect on their choices and possibly lead them to a new perspective.

CHAPTER FORTY-FIVE

PAIN AND PLEASURE

I learned a powerful concept in NLP *(Neuro Linguistic Programming)*: We are the ultimate storytellers in our lives. Nothing has inherent meaning except the meaning we assign to it. Events and people don't come with predefined meanings; we create those meanings ourselves.

For instance, if you associate a particular activity with pain, you will eventually avoid it. You'll find countless reasons to avoid doing it.

Example: The Gym

If you view going to the gym as painful, you'll find a thousand excuses not to go. It might be raining, too hot, you might not have the latest neon shoes, or perhaps you haven't had a haircut and are worried about running into your gym crush. The list of excuses can be endless. You'll find enough reasons to convince yourself that staying cozy under the blanket is a true act of self-love.

For me, it's been two months since I last went to the gym. My current association with the gym is pain, while pleasure is tied to lazing around on the couch. So, how do I reverse this association?

Reversing the Association:

Pleasure:

- If I hit the gym regularly, I'll look fit and feel more confident.
- My gym crush might notice me.
- I'll feel good in the pants I've wanted to wear for a long time.
- People might ask me which college I'm studying at, and I can proudly mention I have two kids.

Pain:

- People might call me "uncle" at a young age.
- Walking up the stairs could become exhausting.
- My performance in bed might suffer.
- I might develop health issues due to a low metabolism.
- I may need to buy two seats on a flight to accommodate myself.

By associating the gym with pleasure and not going with pain, you'll have enough motivation to hit the gym.

You can apply this principle to any area of life. For example, I have promised myself that I will buy a poodle for my family if I release this book. These small associations of pleasure help encourage us to push ourselves and wake up each morning.

Have you seen the image of a donkey being led by a carrot? We are not so different from that donkey. But remember, you are aware of the carrot; if someone else holds it, you might end up in a never-ending cycle.

Take control of your life. Reward yourself for positive actions, and your brain will become wired to seek out and repeat those positive behaviors.

CHAPTER FORTY-SIX

OUR FREEDOM IS NOT OUR OWN

I recently watched a movie called **"Laapata Ladies"**. From start to finish, it was a laughter marathon, but it also highlighted many negative beliefs that women in India still grapple with. This movie is something that women worldwide can relate to, and it's definitely worth watching for men as well.

We often think our freedom is entirely our own, but one thing I realized is that the freedom we enjoy today is the result of many people's efforts. In the movie, Br. Ambedkar's image appears multiple times. It was due to him that the laws in India were reformed and rights were established.

While reflecting on this movie with my wife, we discussed how we are benefiting from the reforms made by individuals who fought for change long before we were born. In India, there were times when people from lower castes were not allowed to wear slippers, and in Kerala, there was a **"Breast tax"** that prohibited lower-caste women from covering their breasts.

How absurd does that sound today? It may seem outrageous now, but it was considered normal at the time. Thanks to those who questioned such practices, significant progress has been made. I'm proud of how Kerala has evolved; you can see it in the quality of movies being produced. Films like **"Great Indian Kitchen"**, **"Jaya Jaya Jaya Hey"**, and **"Archana 31 Not Out"** demonstrate how art can drive societal reform. Art—whether through movies, music, or drama—plays a significant role in shaping and improving society.

This reminds me of the movie **"Cloud Atlas"**. If you haven't seen it, I highly recommend it. If you have, watching it again is still worthwhile. The film illustrates how every event is interconnected across the past, present, and future.

I've been inspired to write a book which explores the insights and lessons that movies have taught me. This idea came to me while writing this chapter. If you think I should pursue it, please let me know in the review for this book :)

Our freedom is not solely our own but is a gift from those who came before us. Let's take a moment to appreciate and thank those individuals who fought for and secured the freedoms we enjoy today.

CHAPTER FORTY-SEVEN

HOW SHOULD WE LIVE?

How should we live? Is success the ultimate goal? Should we aim to get married by 30? Is having a profession essential? Should we have children? What is the correct way to live?

Are there definitive answers to these questions? Even if there are, will they apply universally?

I recommend checking out a guy named Malte Marten on YouTube. His music is extraordinary—truly out of this world. But more importantly, watch his video and you'll understand what I'm about to convey.

Here's my perspective: Malte Marten's approach to life seems to embody living in the moment. He appears to be fully immersed in his art, not fixated on future outcomes or past regrets. Are we too preoccupied with the future, letting our actions be driven by anticipated results? What if we acted not for the sake of outcomes, but simply for the joy of doing?

Children exemplify this. They play not with future goals in mind, but because it brings them joy in the present. Isn't it remarkable how aligned they are with the present moment compared to us? Perhaps we can learn from them how to live fully each day.

Eckhart Tolle, a spiritual author, teaches the importance of living in the present moment in his book **"The Power of Now."** While listening to his speech during a car ride, he mentioned that spirituality isn't something to attain but something to realize.

In other words, we are inherently spiritual; it's the noise of our thoughts that obscures this truth. You don't need to climb mountains or embark on long journeys to discover this. The secret is right here, in the present moment. There's no need to catch a train to reach the present—realize that you're already there.

Returning to our main question: What is the correct way to live? Who decides it for us? Are we constrained by the expectations of others?

The answer to this question is personal and varies from individual to individual. We often try to fit ourselves into predefined boxes, looking at others to see who aligns with our frequency, and attempting to emulate them. While inspiration from others is valuable, finding your own path is crucial.

Both Eckhart Tolle and Rhonda Byrne convey similar concepts, but through their unique styles and experiences.

Remember, everything has already been said in this world, but people seek new perspectives. Sometimes, we forget this. So, express your own voice and determine how you want to live.

Stay in touch with yourself and listen to your inner voice. That's what I learned from observing Malte Marten. I don't believe he copied his style from anyone; rather, he developed his unique voice through his journey.

This book is different from others. I haven't read anything like it, and I'm not trying to teach you per se. Instead, I'm sharing my perspective and aiming to be as authentic as possible. I acknowledge my mistakes and want to present myself as a human being who has written this book. This is my style, found through my own experiences.

My first two books were different, and you can compare them for yourself. Over time, as years have passed, my original voice has come to the forefront. I tried to fit into several boxes, but it was uncomfortable.

Now, I ask you: How do you wish to live?

CHAPTER FORTY-EIGHT

WHAT IS YOUR BEST WORK?

I've mentioned the legend Suki Sivam in my previous book and this one as well, but his teachings are too profound to overlook. Suki Sivam has shared many gems in Tamil, one of the world's oldest languages.

In one of his speeches, he was asked, *"What was the best speech you've given to date?"* His response was, **"My next speech."** How brilliant is that? He went on to explain that after receiving awards and national recognition, it's easy to let ego take over, convincing ourselves that we are the greatest. That's where our downfall begins.

When we do good work, it's tempting to think we can't surpass it. However, I believe in the philosophy of *"Improve a bit more."* This mindset isn't limited to professionals or those in serious careers. If you meditate for 10 minutes a day, extend it to 12 minutes. If you've mastered 12 minutes, increase it to 15 minutes. Just a little more.

As Martin Luther King Jr. said, **"If you can't fly, then run.**

If you can't run, then walk. If you can't walk, then crawl, but by all means, keep moving."

I strive to implement this philosophy in my own work. I believe this book is more advanced than my first, and once I finish it, my next book should be even better. I'll look to famous authors, read new books, and expand my awareness. Just because my previous book was a success doesn't mean I can rest on my laurels.

This progressive mindset keeps us alive and active. Consider how you can apply this in your life:

- Can you be a bit more mindful in your work?
- Can you spend a little more time with a friend?
- Can you walk an extra 500 steps today?
- Can you be a bit more grateful in your life?
- Can you smile a bit more at those around you?
- Can you post an honest review for a book you're currently enjoying? :)

There is always room for improvement. Look for it today, and see how it can make a difference in your life.

CHAPTER FORTY-NINE

EVERYTHING CAN BE YOUR TEACHER

You might think that only schools and colleges can teach you something, but even the smallest things around you can offer valuable lessons. An insect, a rain shower, or even a simple drive can be great teachers. There's an old saying: ***"The teacher appears only when the student is ready."*** I used to think this meant a physical person would show up as a teacher, but I was wrong. The real teacher is within us. No one can teach us anything if we're not open to learning.

Recently, while driving back to my hometown, I listened to a podcast where Suki Sivam discussed the lessons he learned from cricket. His insights were so intriguing that I thought you might benefit from them too. He used cricket as a metaphor for life, and his perspective was both enlightening and entertaining.

Imagine a cricket match as a reflection of life. In this

analogy, the bowler is constantly delivering deliveries aimed at challenging you, while you, as the batsman, are trying to score runs from these deliveries. Life is full of challenges, and just like in cricket, these challenges can be turned into opportunities if we approach them correctly.

In a cricket match, it's not just the bowler who's trying to get you out. There are also ten fielders positioned around the ground, each one ready to catch the ball or stop it from reaching the boundary, all with the aim of getting you out. This reflects the various obstacles and pressures we face in life, often from people or situations around us.

Then there's the crowd watching the game. These spectators are like distant relatives who may have little real involvement in our personal lives but still have plenty to say. Sivam describes these onlookers as people who might not be actively contributing to their own lives. They might cheer or criticize, but their opinions shouldn't sway you.

If you become overly focused on the applause or criticism from the crowd, you risk losing concentration on the real challenge ahead. Just as in cricket, where you need to stay focused on the bowler and not be distracted by the crowd, you must remain focused on your own path and not be overly influenced by external validation. Letting either praise or criticism affect you too much can lead to mistakes.

Suki Sivam concluded his talk by emphasizing that the teacher is everywhere. When you become truly aware of yourself and your surroundings, you'll find that lessons appear all around you. Life itself becomes a series of teachings. It's up to you to recognize and learn from these lessons.

So, the next time you face a challenge or encounter an unexpected situation, remember that it might be a lesson in disguise. Stay open to learning from every experience, no matter how small or seemingly insignificant. This mindset will help you grow and adapt, turning everyday moments into valuable lessons.

CHAPTER FIFTY

LIFE LESSONS OR LIFE INTERPRETATIONS

Sometimes, it feels as though life is teaching us important lessons.

But does life really teach us, or are we simply interpreting events based on our own situations?

We are, after all, pattern recognition machines. We want everything to make sense, so we observe and draw conclusions based on what we see. Yet, in reality, nothing is inherently meaningful—it's the interpretation we give to it that makes it so.

In quantum reality, there's a concept that a particle exists in a superposition state and only takes on a definite state when observed. This suggests that the observer influences the state by their expectations.

Perhaps, then, events are just events, without intrinsic

meaning. It's we who associate them with life lessons, like the ones in this book.

Maybe I saw these 50 lessons in the real world because I was looking for them. Perhaps they were just random occurrences, and my pattern-seeking brain organized them into coherent lessons that made sense to me.

So, don't take any of this to heart—none of this is an absolute truth, just my interpretations of life. Live your own life, experience your own events, and seek out your own answers.

After all, the meaning you find in life is uniquely yours to discover.